Write Like a Pro

Ten Techniques for Getting Your Point Across at Work (and in Life)

Carl Hausman

 PRAEGER™

An Imprint of ABC-CLIO, LLC

Santa Barbara, California • Denver, Colorado

Library of Congress Cataloging-in-Publication Data

Names: Hausman, Carl, 1953– author.
Title: Write like a pro : ten techniques for getting your point across at
    work (and in life) / Carl Hausman.
Description: Santa Barbara : Praeger, [2016] | Includes bibliographical references and index.
Identifiers: LCCN 2015046508 | ISBN 9781440844140 (hardback) |
    ISBN 9781440844157 (ebook) | ISBN 9781440850646 (paperback)
Subjects: LCSH: English language—Business English—Self-instruction. | Business writing—
    Study and teaching. | Business writing—Self-instruction. | BISAC: BUSINESS &
    ECONOMICS / Business Writing.
Classification: LCC PE1115 .H39 2016 | DDC 808/.042—dc23
LC record available at http://lccn.loc.gov/2015046508

ISBN: 978-1-4408-4414-0 (hardcover)
ISBN: 978-1-4408-5064-6 (paperback)
EISBN: 978-1-4408-4415-7

20 19 18 17 16   1 2 3 4 5

This book is also available on the World Wide Web as an eBook.
Visit www.abc-clio.com for details.

Praeger
An Imprint of ABC-CLIO, LLC

ABC-CLIO, LLC
130 Cremona Drive, P.O. Box 1911
Santa Barbara, California 93116–1911

This book is printed on acid-free paper ∞

Manufactured in the United States of America

Contents

Expanded Contents

Introduction

OK, let's put our cards on the table.

You're reading this introduction for the only reason anyone ever reads introductions—to figure out whether you want to buy this book.

And the reason I'm writing the introduction, of course, is to get you to buy the book.

So here's my pitch: I can make you a better writer, and I have a simple, uncluttered, no-BS method to do it. I've perfected this method after decades of turning out more than a dozen books and thousands of articles and columns. (Google me. Buy all my other books. Thanks.) In addition, I've polished my packaging and delivery of this method during a long career as a journalism professor.

While this book is in large part designed for readers who want to burnish their skills in business writing, I believe writers of all genres can transform their prose with these techniques. To a great extent, *writing is writing.*

And there's nothing mysterious about the process. Learning how to write well is simply absorbing and repeating a technique. Technique itself is just a means to an end: You can learn karate and discover how to punch out a mugger, or you can study writing and excel in the workplace, persuade others to adopt your point of view, and communicate your passions.

Karate and writing are both excellent pursuits, but without strong writing *you'll be mugged by life.*

You will inevitably suffer the frustrations of having your message blunted and your thoughts ignored.

So, how can my ten-point approach help? Well, I've organized the principles of elegant writing into ten basic techniques. Each technique is explained in ten sets of instructions. When appropriate, which it usually is, I include an example clearly demonstrating how the principle being discussed has been used by an accomplished writer to great effect.

But why my obsession with ten? I believe that as humans we are hard-wired to think and absorb in increments of ten. Our number system is based on ten, no doubt due to the original meaning of the word "digital" (relating to the finger, the device that has helped me overcome math challenges for many years).

There are ten commandments, ten amendments in the Bill of Rights, a boxer is knocked out after a count of ten, and the mathematician Pythagoras not only figured out some high school formula that as I recall has something to do with triangles but also theorized that ten was the symbol of numerical perfection and was the embodiment of the universe.

The Romans virtually based their social order on the number ten, with a leader of ten reporting to another leader of ten groups, and so on. The Latin word for a leader of ten was *decan*, from the same root that provides the word "decade," and the concept of a group leader in church being a "deacon" and in a college being a "dean."

If you're not yet convinced, take a look at the table of contents. Notice the advice given in the first two items: *Before writing, determine how what you're going to say meets the needs of the reader and how those needs mesh with what you want to accomplish*. That's exactly what I did in the opening of this introduction. I also quickly arrayed some evidence on why I was qualified to write this book and how the information herein could provide you with a tangible benefit, the second technique explained in the book. Note that I followed my own advice and used strong, interesting, and compelling verbs—like "arrayed"—and ladled in a little humor to keep you from going to sleep.

Note, too, that you are still reading.

So now that I'm through patting myself on the back, let's get started.

How to Use This Book

You can access this book in any order you like (after all, you now own it), but I'd recommend starting at the beginning and reading it straight through. The 100 steps are presented in what I have calculated to be a need-to-know sequence. In other words, the most important and fundamental steps for raising your writing to a professional level are presented first, with refinements to the fundamentals following in order of importance and usefulness.

I've tried to keep cross-referencing to a minimum because it can become distracting, but in many cases I do refer you to another section, sometimes for related advice or reassurance that a more advanced application of the instructions will be expanded upon later. References to steps in other chapters will cite both chapter and step, for example, Chapter 2, Step 7. References to numbered steps within the same chapter will simply cite the step number: Step 7.

There are brief examples used in most of the steps, some real and some composed by me for precise illustration of a technique. The book concludes with a selection of effective pieces and, through commentary, I show how some of the techniques have been put into practice by others.

The focus of the book is how to write elegantly, convincingly, and expressively—the caliber of writing that is adaptable to any writing task. As I stress throughout the book, there's no longer any strict segregation between journalism, business writing, blog composition, social media posting, and so forth. The era of digital convergence has baked all those disciplines into the same cake.

As a result, I'm not going to be explaining "How to Format a Memo," or any other pedestrian task you can learn with a web search. I also won't be offering a course in remedial English, because if you need that type of intervention you should start with a different book. However, I do point out the more common grammar mistakes that writers, even highly educated and experienced ones, frequently make, and I give clear advice on how to avoid such errors. (English is a complex and irregular language and everybody makes mistakes, but I provide some easy-to-remember guidelines.) I won't be swooning over the intricacies of literary symbolism, either. Having said that, I do include some examples from Shakespeare: Remember, he was a clever stylist who needed to keep the attention of audiences who were often working-class, so there are plenty of engaging tricks he has to offer us.

Much of the focus in the book is on what you might call "tricks" or, more accurately, "devices" and "techniques." Don't be put off by this approach. Every high-level professional employs mechanics. Opera singers learn to produce more volume by pushing their abdomens upward. Baseball players learn to throw harder by taking a longer stride. Comedians learn to get a bigger laugh by pausing a beat before the punch line.

So with that said, here are the ten techniques, each laid out in ten sequential steps, that will elevate your writing to a new level.

Chapter 1

Deploy a Professional Writer's Strategy to Produce Engaging, Powerful, and Persuasive Writing—and Do It on a Schedule

Amateurish writing is often misbegotten at birth: Its purpose is unclear and therefore does not engage the reader or make the appropriate point. It is disorganized, uninteresting, and cobbled together haphazardly—often at the last minute and in a state of panic. Here is how professionals avoid that trap by determining an initial approach and organizing the piece and the workflow.

STEP 1: DECIDE WHAT'S IN IT FOR THE READER

As a professional writer, your first responsibility is to provide your readers with a benefit. (You *are* a professional, by the way. If any part of your job involves writing, you're getting paid for it and thus enjoy professional status. If you *want* to write books, blogs, or articles for a living and are engaged in self-education through this book, you're *still* a pro—an emerging professional who is waiting, like many businesspeople do, for the return on investment.)

Remember that the fundamental purpose of a professional is to provide clients with something they need. A doctor gives you a cure for your headache, and your accountant wades through your incomprehensible forms to help you pay the least tax possible. And a lawyer keeps you out of jail if you're not exactly honest with your accountant.

The benefit you, as a writer, are providing might not initially appear so clear-cut, but I'll bet you can precisely define it after a little thought. The benefit might be:

> *I want to make the division head reading this report comfortable in granting my department the increased budget I'm asking for.*
>
> -or-
>
> *I want to entertain my reader and leave that reader feeling a little bit smarter, saying, "wow—I never thought of it that way."*

I wrote those examples carefully to illustrate a couple of key points.

You'll notice I didn't define the benefit in the first example as "I want to get more money," or "I want the reader to like my article." There is nothing wrong with wanting something for your direct benefit (see the next entry), but ultimately *the appeal for what you want has to be filtered through the lens of the person who can give you what you want.*

This is a profound point, if I do say so myself, and alone it is worth the price of the book. However, rest assured that I will write the rest of the book anyway.

Again, remember that what you want is irrelevant to the reader. Your job is to give the reader what he or she wants and needs. By giving that to the reader, you get what you want.

Here is an example. In one of my forays into the corporate world I once wrote a very long and detailed document asking for more resources for the department where I worked. I wanted more resources, but was well aware that the division head reading the document had no interest in what I wanted. The division head would be reading my report looking for reasons to give a limited amount of resources to one department and not another. She had to; it was a zero-sum game and some departments had to wind up with little or nothing.

So, the question was not "what do I want," but, "how can I help the reader make and ultimately justify the decision to her bosses?"

The approach worked, by the way—and I heard through the grapevine that the person holding the purse strings liked the way I had provided her the ammunition she needed to craft a budget that favored me.

About the second example of a benefit to the reader: *I want to entertain my reader and leave that reader feeling a little bit smarter, saying, "wow—I never thought of it that way."* Virtually all readers, including me, want to be entertained, even if the primary purpose of the piece is not amusement. I also love picking up insights and tidbits of interesting information—perhaps to re-inflict them on someone at tonight's cocktail party.

Moral: If I want the reader to like (and consume) my writing, I do my best to give the reader what he or she wants.

Note that in this section I've made several tedious and oddly constructed references to "the reader" instead of "readers." I won't do that from now on because it's too grammatically awkward to keep torturing sentences into the singular (see Chapter 5, Step 3), but it's crucial to realize that even though many people may read your writing, *individuals*—not groups—consume the work. You are communicating with one person at a time, and should never let your writing assume the air of something destined for "all of you out there."

STEP 2: DECIDE WHAT'S IN IT FOR YOU

There's really no point in writing anything unless it produces a benefit to you. By that, I don't necessarily mean monetary or professional gain. Your benefit might be simply venting or writing for pleasure. Writing for the sake of writing can be therapeutic; you don't need a second person in the transaction if you are writing a diary and gain some clarity and insight by organizing your thoughts on the page.

Some writers are motivated entirely by personal gain—say, the notion that one will make a lot of money by writing a derivative book that cashes in on a hot trend. That's a perfectly valid motive, although "cashing in" doesn't usually work out that well. If your heart and head really are not in the subject, it's hard to write about it well, and by the time most people see the results of a trend the trend has already peaked.

No motive is entirely a bad motive. The issue is whether you're being honest with yourself so you can proceed in the direction that will benefit you.

What's your motive? Your desired result?

- I want people to think I am indescribably clever
- I want to get a raise
- I want to show that the person who disagrees with me is a baboon
- I want the person reading my instructions to understand exactly what to do (and keep me out of trouble)
- I want people to understand and sympathize with my point of view

- I want to calm down a person who is complaining
- I want to inspire people to love my topic as much as I do
- I want to establish myself as an expert in this particular field
- I want to show that I am as smart or smarter than the people I work with

None of these is inherently a good or bad reason. The important thing is to know, acknowledge, and pursue your real desired result, both in the short term and in the long term.

The desired result is the spine of your writing, the backbone that keeps it upright and moving. Whatever doesn't support, fortify, or stick to it will weaken your presentation and must be trimmed away.

To put it another way: You have to identify what it is that you want to accomplish and write in such a way that the reader sees a benefit to going along with the process. It's not a complicated process, and it doesn't require soul-searching or meditation on a mountaintop—just a few minutes' thought and some common sense.

STEP 3: IDENTIFY ONE CENTRAL THOUGHT

You have to decide what your piece is about and clearly telegraph it to the reader, and then you have to confine yourself to writing about what you promised.

A memo, article, blog post, or any piece of writing that doesn't have a perceptible main focus is not going to hold the reader's attention or attract that attention in the first place. Readers are fickle. They'll lose interest in a flash if confused or bored, and if the point of your work is unclear or meanders, you'll drive them away. Even if it's something they are compelled to read, such as a report, you'll subtly antagonize them by injecting friction into the writing/reading transaction and their interest, retention, and pliability will be eroded.

In addition to *identifying* the central thought, you have to tell the reader what it is. Summarize it, or at least refer to it, near the beginning of your piece.

The part of your writing that tells the reader what the piece is about is called the lead. There are two basic types of leads, *direct leads* and *indirect leads*. I'm not using the terms synonymously with journalistic leads, which sometimes follow a somewhat-arcane format, but there are many similarities.

For our purposes, just think of a lead as a preview of what is coming.

For a **direct lead**, simply summarize what's ahead and then use the following paragraph to amplify. You'll notice that's exactly what I did in the first sentence of this entry and the next paragraph. That was *a direct lead* to the central thought.

I summarized what was coming:

> *You have to decide what your piece is about and clearly telegraph it to the reader, and then you have to confine yourself to writing about what you promised.*

And then amplified:

> *A memo, article, blog post, or any piece of writing that doesn't have a perceptible main focus is not going to hold the reader's attention or attract that attention in the first place. Readers are fickle. They'll lose interest in a flash if confused or bored, and if the point of your work is unclear or meanders you'll drive them away. Even if it's something they are compelled to read, such as a report, you'll subtly antagonize them by injecting friction into the writing/ reading transaction and their interest, retention, and pliability will be eroded.*

The **indirect lead** builds up a little suspense in the opening line or paragraph, sometimes utilizing a tease that captures the readers' attention and leading them into the following part—the part that identifies the central thought.

Feature (newspaper and magazine soft-news) writers use the indirect lead to capture attention and pull the reader into the story. For example, I once was assigned to write an article about rugby, an unfamiliar, somewhat-violent, and always-raucous British sport that was beginning to make some headway in the United States and the Boston area in particular. I focused on one team in Worcester, Massachusetts, to tell the story.

The central thought is pretty clear:

> *Rugby is an up-and-coming sport, but it's confusing, strange to the American eye, quite violent and very raucous. There's a team right here that is competing in a league that's part of a national league structure, and they are doing pretty well. Here is their story.*

The central thought is fairly complex and boring, at least the way it's stated here.

So I used the indirect lead to segue into the central thought, opening with an attention-grabbing tease followed by the paragraphs that summed up what's coming.

> *Michael Minty learned his sport as a youth in his native Wembley, England. He came home from one of his first games with two black eyes, seven stitches*

above one eyebrow, a swollen lip, and a torn nostril. His father looked up from the dinner table: "Been playing rugby, have you?"

Then the second paragraph sets the road map for the central thought and how the central thought will progress through the article:

Minty, not one to be easily discouraged, is today player-coach of the Worcester Rugby Football club, established two years ago. Competing in what's called the B Division of the New England Rugby Union . . . [I follow with more detail, including the team's 13–11 winning record . . . then the next paragraph notes that the record is quite respectable because two-thirds of the team never played the game before the team was assembled . . . and then comes the requisite detail about broken bones and wild parties.]

Once you've established the central thought, keep everything that follows somehow related to it. Journalists call this "supporting your lead." This is important. Don't wander off track.

The process of writing is truly enjoyable. Many people find AHA! DID YOU NOTICE I JUST WENT OFF TRACK AND LOST YOU? The central thought of this entry is:

A memo, article, blog post—anything—that doesn't have a perceptible main focus is a loser. Readers are fickle. They'll lose interest in a flash if confused or bored, and if the point of your work is unclear or meanders you'll drive them away. . . .

And the stuff about writing being enjoyable is not relevant to this entry and thus doesn't follow the lead and thus must be euthanized.

We'll focus on paragraphing and transitions in Chapter 2 of this book, but at this point remember that if *what you have in the piece doesn't follow your lead, get rid of it.* If what you have to excise is absolutely essential, then your lead is written incorrectly and should be revised.

STEP 4: BREAK YOUR THOUGHT INTO A FEW MAIN CHUNKS

You'll save yourself frustration and avoid false starts if you make an initial outline of how you want to express your central thought. The outline can be rudimentary or detailed; the point is that you need to determine the main sections of your piece before you start writing it.

Let's use a business-related scenario: You are a corporate communications executive and want to start an online internal newsletter for your firm, and need an OK from the board of directors and a budget for the project. You want to start the newsletter because you believe it will bring long-term benefits: a more congenial workplace and higher annual profits.

Notice that you've just clarified your **central thought:**

> *You want to start an online newsletter for your firm because you believe the benefits will pay off in the long run, both in terms of a better workplace and the bottom line.*

By the way, to echo the first two points in this book, you've just clarified **what's in it for the reader (Step 1):** When writing this memo to the board, you are certainly going to stress the bottom-line benefits. Profit is what a board of directors is responsible for maintaining.

What's in it for you (Step 2)? If your job is in corporate communications, you're expanding your reach within the organization, possibly adding an employee or two, and increasing your status within the firm (assuming your idea works).

You've established what's in it for the reader and for you, and identified your one central thought. Now, what are the main chunks of what you want to communicate?

You think it's a good idea because the company needs better communication, which will provide . . .

- a morale boost,
- a place to get accurate knowledge about the firm,
- a vehicle to reinforce company policies, and
- a venue where management can dispel rumors.

The newsletter will cost, let's say, $100,000 per year, but you believe the project will more than pay for itself by stemming recent defections (hiring and training new employees is expensive) and stave off a few personnel issues that have cost time and money.

You need resources to get the project under way, and you've scoped out what you will request.

Answering that question was easy. And now, you've broken up your central through into nine main chunks:

1. Need a newsletter
2. Why? Need better communication
3. Newsletter would provide morale boost
4. Newsletter would be a place to provide accurate knowledge about what's happening in the company
5. Newsletter could deal with, explain, and reinforce company policies

6. Can dispel rumors
7. Will cost $100,000
8. Will pay for itself by limiting turnover of staff and lawsuits
9. We need A, B, C, and D in resources to make it work

Now you know what goes into the recipe. Next, it's a simple exercise to figure out the order in which the ingredients are mixed.

STEP 5: ARRANGE THE CHUNKS INTO A BEGINNING, MIDDLE, AND END

You've got nine chunks that make up the sum total of what you want to communicate. Put the chunks in the order that makes sense, and you've got an **outline.**

What's the strategy of making this outline? If I were you, I'd avoid asking for the money at the outset. I would make my case first, implying that I am not asking for money but rather offering a *solution.* (Chapter 7 deals with techniques of persuasion, but here let me simply invoke an old salesman's bromide: "Don't sell drills, sell holes.")

Also, if I had a good story to tell at the beginning, I would probably use an indirect lead. Suppose, for example, there had been a recent spate of defections of top account executives who left for greener pastures because they believed that the company was going to cut back the sales force—an assumption based on rumor that was not true.

Like the example of the rugby player with the torn nostril (can you get the image for a torn nostril out of your head?) this opening makes a memorable point.

Next, I would make my basic statement of what the memo is about and preview what's coming. I would emphasize the point that if the newsletter had existed, it would be likely that the account executives would not have defected.

That's one benefit of the proposed newsletter—a good starting point for ticking off the other benefits.

Following that, I would describe the resources needed, conclude with the pitch for the $100,000, and refer back to the story with which I opened the memo. (That's an old writer's trick called starting in the middle and ending at the beginning; more on that strategy follows in the next entry.)

Here, then, is the outline:

- Story of defections
- Why we need newsletter—stop rumor and provide other benefits that will be good for the bottom line

- Benefits include overall better communication
- Why better communication is a benefit

  ○ As stated, dispels rumors
  ○ Provides accurate knowledge
  ○ Provides morale boost by helping people know each other and firm
  ○ Helps people understand policies—and avoid incidents like the two harassment cases that cost us tens of thousands in legal bills last year

- Resources needed
- Budget needed
- Conclusion—Let's save money and frustration by heading off problems before they start . . . let's not lose any more employees because of unfounded rumor or lawsuits because employees did not understand policy

STEP 6: IF POSSIBLE, START IN THE MIDDLE AND END AT THE BEGINNING

"Starting in the middle" means begin your piece with action, something relevant and attention-grabbing. You won't always be able to invoke this strategy, but it works more often than you might expect. In the newsletter example, we started with a story about the defections. It galvanized interest, drove the reader to the next point, and reinforced the main idea.

Crime novelist Lawrence Block, who is also a renowned teacher of writing, is an advocate of this principle. He once recounted a problem he had with a book he was writing: It seemed tedious when the central character recounted the motivations for the murder, the plotting, and the eventual disposal of the body—not an easy task in New York City. The murderer was strong and the victim small, so he rolled the body up in a carpet and carried it on his shoulder on the subway. But all that planning and plotting was a snooze.

The solution: *Start the book with a guy on the subway carrying a body wrapped in a carpet.*

Really, how could you NOT turn the next page after that opening? Moral: Start in the middle if you reasonably can. Draw the reader in.

And when possible, end at the beginning. This simply means circle back to your opening statement or story. (Stories are usually called "anecdotes" when we refer to them in the context of nonfiction writing.) Some sort of reference back to the beginning serves as sort of "I told you so" and also makes the piece seem spherical and complete.

For example, let's say you're writing an article about a business manager who decided to quit his corporate job to pursue his dream and go to medical school.

Start the story in the middle, with some action that *tells the story:*

> *When Bob Hastings, the head of a seven-person accounting department, was told he'd have to lay some people off, he decided that he wanted to help people, not hurt them, so he fired himself.*

Then summarize the main idea:

> *Hastings, 33 at the time, joined a growing trend of mid-career workers who enter medical school older but wiser than their fellow students. . .*

Then tell the whole story however you'd like, using more anecdotes, examples, and quotes, following your outline. To give the story some punch, and make it seem complete, *end at the beginning:*

> *When Hastings graduated last year, he didn't expect to see anyone at the ceremony. He had no spouse or nearby family. But he was astounded to see that waiting to shake his hand were all seven members of his old department—the people he'd refused to fire.*

Not all written works will adapt themselves to this type of circular ending, but you'd be surprised how many will if you pay attention and look for the right material.

STEP 7: DETERMINE THE APPROPRIATE TONE

The tenor of the writing is as important as the content. You'll have to use your judgment to decide at what level the piece will communicate. Then, maintain the same tone throughout the entire piece.

"Tone" is a rather abstract concept, difficult to define and even harder to dictate. However, you can instinctively gauge tone by reading other pieces and noting the way they communicate. And you can easily craft your own tone by emulating the pieces that strike a chord that resonates with you. Make a mental note when you read an effective column, blog, internal communication, or other work. What was the tone and why did it work?

When discussing tone, it's easier to define what it should *not* be than what it should be.

Here are some guidelines about what to avoid:

- **Do not make your tone stilted and academic.** Wooden phrases like "We strive to maintain . . ." are pretentious, awkward, and betray an amateur trying to "strive" to appear smarter than he or she really is. Writing "we will interface to collaborate for a positive outcome" doesn't make you seem important or a master strategist. It implies you are intellectually insecure and need to lard your writing with the trappings of intellect but not the evidence of intellect.

- **Don't be flip or sarcastic, unless you want to be perceived that way and are capable of pulling it off.** Sarcasm is an art and misfires more often than not. Writing "And we all know how that worked out, haha" or "Yeah, good luck with that . . ." will brand you as a dimwitted malcontent. More sophisticated sarcasm can work, but it must be wielded deftly, and that takes a great deal of skill and an in-depth knowledge of your reader's sensibilities. Be careful of humor in general, although the right type of humor—generally gentle and self-deprecating—can magnetically engage the reader. (See Chapter 4, Step 8.)
- **Be careful of anger.** Expressions of outrage appear particularly severe when entombed forever on the page, usually much more starkly than what you meant. You may have written an angry or sarcastic sentence with a smile, but the reader has no way of perceiving your mood other than by the blunt wording.
- **Avoid being too chummy.** Excessive familiarity in writing is more distasteful than an overly familiar approach in person. Unlike face-to-face encounters, you have no way of dialing back an off-putting tone if the person on the receiving end reacts negatively. Maintain a decorous distance. Go easy on the in-jokes, and don't assume that every reader shares your worldview.
- **Having said all of the above: Strike a balance that avoids stiff formality.** In most circumstances you can use contractions, refer to the reader in the second person ("You may have encountered this situation last year, when . . ."), and refer to yourself as "I." You're in the business of communicating human-to-human, and dialing down the formality a notch usually makes your message more accessible.

STEP 8: COLLECT AND TRANSCRIBE YOUR MATERIALS TOGETHER ON STANDARD-SIZE PAPER (NO NAPKINS, MATCHBOOKS, POST-IT NOTES, OR YOUTUBE VIDEOS)

Long writing projects are intimidating not only because of the amount of work involved but also because it's challenging to manage the mass of materials you have gathered in the research process. And if you have a disorganized pile of sources, it exacerbates the dilemma of deciding what goes where when you are constructing the piece.

I have a two-step system that has seen me through several hundred articles and more than a dozen books. It works for me, I think it will work for you as well, and it certainly can't hurt to try.

The first step is to get all your source materials organized in a manageable and accessible collection. The second step is to write up an outline of your project and then key it to your source material—labeling what part from your source material goes where in the outline.

Type up your handwritten notes neatly on however many pages you need and print them out. Transcribe them quickly after you take your notes, because if your handwriting is like mine what looks legible today won't be so clear tomorrow and in a week it will look like hieroglyphics viewed in a mirror after a pitcher of vodka martinis. Transcribing your notes also allows you to edit out unnecessary material.

If you have pages from a book or magazine, photocopy them onto standard-size paper. Print out the relevant parts of web pages you want to cite.

Now, instead of a heap of books, magazines, notebooks, scrawled-upon napkins, web bookmarks, and matchbook covers, you have a neat sheaf of pages. I like to hole-punch them and insert them into a binder. Number the pages at the top in red marker and you're ready for the next step.

STEP 9: KEY YOUR SOURCES TO YOUR OUTLINE—A FIVE-MINUTE PROCESS THAT WILL SAVE YOU HOURS OR DAYS OF TRIAL AND ERROR

After you collect and transcribe your notes, create an outline of your document. The length and detail will vary depending on the nature of the work and how much time you want to spend planning at this stage.

For purposes of this example, let's use just the first three points of a hypothetical (and vague) outline. So, the beginning of your outline might look like this . . .

1. Introduction
2. Explanation of why the issue is important
3. First example

. . . and so on.

Print your outline.

Next, put your *source documents* in one pile to your left and your *outline* to the right.

Now, the magic happens. Go through your source documents and pick out the good parts. Underline (or highlight) and label them. Let's say on Page 1 of your source document you have a quote that you think is powerful and evocative. Underline it, and then take your red marker and label it "A" in the right-hand column of the page. The quote is now coded as Page 1, Paragraph A.

A little farther down on Page 1 of the source documents you may have some statistics that you believe will back up an important contention in your piece. Label that paragraph as "B."

Do this throughout all your source pages. All the good parts will be identified: *Source Page 1, paragraphs A, B, C, D, Source Page 2, paragraphs A, B, C, D, E,* and so forth.

Now turn your attention to the outline. Look at it carefully and think about *what* information from your source documents should go *where*. Under each of your ten main points in the outline, write in the code for the sections of your source documents that you want to use.

Using the hypothetical "Introduction" section in the outline as at example, you may wind up with something like this:

Outline Point 1: Introduction

(Use this information from the source documents . . .)

Page 2, paragraph C
Page 1, paragraph A
Page 8, paragraph D
Page 1, paragraph F
Page 1, paragraph G

You can create this outline/roadmap on the computer screen if you want, but using a printed version works best for me and doesn't tie up valuable real estate on my computer screen. Some source documents you will want to access in electronic form. If I have a quote I want to copy and paste from my source documents, for example, I can always go back to the electronic version of the documents and copy it from there. But I still go through the ritual of printing it out and keeping it in my source pile.

Give my method a try. It really does make the task physically and psychologically easier—making writing a long article or report more like responding to essay questions when you already know the answer.

Again, I must stress that an outline is a tremendous help. If you're allergic to detailed planning, be assured that even jotting down five entries will channel your mind in the right direction.

If you have a large, complex piece, the outline, which you will eventually key to your notes, can impose a structure on the piece that not only helps with organization but readability, allowing you to think through the approach and make the work complete, spherical, non-repetitive, and packed with good quotes and scenes.

I used this approach when I was assigned to write a long biographical piece about film and camera pioneer George Eastman. Some of what I wrote is cited in Chapter 8, Step 2, the section on using anecdotes to tell a story, and the entire piece is reprinted in Chapter 11. Here I want to focus on the outline.

I had to cover a lot of ground and integrate research from his papers, handwritten notes, references from books and old journals, and an interview with Henry Clune, an elderly newspaperman who had, early in his career, known an aging Eastman.

There were many things I wanted to say in the article, but I had to first identify a central thought. After poring over the source materials, it came to me: The central thought was that Eastman had changed all of American industry in ways that reflected his personal quirkiness. Part of this notion was that Eastman was a product of his times and his ideas developed in an era when the changing nation was ready to accept them; he methodically created his company at a time when method was not particularly in vogue, and he was instrumental in developing the (then) novel idea of corporate philanthropy. All of these accomplishments related to the central idea.

The Eastman profile was the first thing of such scope I had written. After groping down several blind alleys trying to write without any clear structure, I decided to create an outline.

It didn't take me more than an hour. I knew what I had to work with and more or less what I wanted to say, so I took a pen and yellow legal pad and came up with this:

Eastman Outline

1. **Suicide note—strange nature of man**
2. **Theme—why strange nature translated into business success**

   a. Methodical
   b. Structure was an invention
   c. Examples

3. **Transition to background**
4. **Show why background—Eastman's and country's—is important to story**

   a. Inventions
   b. Industrial Revolution

5. **Transition from inventions in general to film**

   a. Problem

   b. Solution to wet plate—use funny letter "intimate"

6. **Question back to theme—method, "knowledge all empirical"**
7. **Bring in birth of consumer technology—only a professional could cope (Brady example)**
8. **Eastman sets mind to find solution**
9. **Background—no scientific training, maybe a good thing**

   a. Research in kitchen

   b. Driven to overcome poverty . . . foreshadow future philanthropy

10. **His research**

    a. More kitchen experiments

    b. Calculating, quality control

    c. Foreshadow mass production idea . . . letter

11. **Breakthrough**
12. **Disaster!**

    a. What he did—make good

    b. Why important—changed nature of business

13. **Once established, where business went . . .**

    a. Film—invention of substance and use of word

    b. Detective camera

    c. Marketing to consumer

    d. Establishment of name KODAK . . . how tied into marketing

    e. More innovation—

       1. Plastic base for film

       2. Funny ivory story—invention of celluloid

    f. Right up to turn of century, close out discussion with reference to society as in open

14. **Product story finished—return to Eastman's personality, what it would mean for closing days of company**

    a. Relationships with women—cold

    b. Clune story and quote—cold

15. **But he began to change (show movement toward end of story)**

    a. Employee benefits

    b. Music—funny Eastman house story

    c. Eastman School of Music

    d. Medical care—childhood trauma

    e. Travel

16. **His declining days—Clune story, show clearly it's near the end**

17. Conclusion

a. Didn't invent a lot of stuff, but did invent consumer technology
b. Relate back to historical material, whole country, in beginning and middle of story
c. Moral of story: He invented consumer technology
d. His was a story where "every revolution was once a thought in one person's mind, and when it occurred to others, it was the key to an era"

Please read through the story in Chapter 11. You can not only see how the story follows the outline, but also how the first nine points of this book were put into practice.

Specifically, I decided what was in it for the reader: an entertaining read that had detail that would allow the reader to connect the dots, as I did when researching the story, among developments in a seminal time in the history of technology.

I decided what was in it for me: The piece would be a new career path for me, mixing humor, "I didn't know that" detail, and a strong narrative that connected different ideas. That's the trajectory I am still following.

I identified one central thought: Eastman had changed American industry in ways that reflected his personal quirkiness.

There were a few main chunks that would tell the story: He was a product of his times and his ideas developed at a time when the changing nation was ready to accept them, how he methodically created his company, and how he was instrumental in developing the (then) novel idea of corporate philanthropy.

I expanded and arranged those chunks into a beginning, middle, and end, and made those bones the skeleton of the outline.

I started in the middle with action: Eastman shot himself, leaving a suicide note that said, "My work is done—why wait?" His method of suicide—he'd asked his doctor to point out the location of his heart—was an indicator of the strange and methodical nature of the man, and was a great introduction to the narrative. I ended at the beginning, circling back to how Eastman's then-strange ideas had become standard practice in industry.

I wanted to pitch the tone at a level similar to other writers who explored technology and popular culture. I chose Carl Sagan and James Burke, both of whom wrote informally and enthusiastically, and clearly were enjoying the connections they unearthed along the way.

Writing the story would be a straightforward task after I collated the source material and keyed it to the outline.

But first I had to get started—the problem we all face as writers. The next technique solves that problem.

STEP 10: WRITE THE DAMN THING *NOW*—HERE'S HOW

The most important step in writing is *writing*. You need to get a draft down on paper and then revise. (We'll cover the revision process in various sections of this book.)

Your primary enemy is procrastination, a particularly difficult problem for writers, which is why I put off writing about it until the end of this chapter.

Everybody has a natural inclination to postpone a challenging task, but we as writers face a particularly onerous set of obstacles because we have to slog through the job and be creative at the same time. We are compelled to prod our minds at bayonet-point to come up with an intriguing lead, cover the requisite facts in a coherent fashion, and produce what is often a dauntingly large chunk of prose.

Here are three techniques to overcome the inertia that keeps us from starting and progressing on a writing project:

- **Begin with the Second or Third Paragraph.** We wordsmiths demand of ourselves the unrelenting ability to craft leads that are inventive, compelling, and, of course, excruciatingly clever. And then we beat ourselves up when we can't deliver and subsequently dither and procrastinate while we wait for our muse. Here's a cure for that. Instead of sweating out dozens of false starts and freezing in fear and frustration while you await the arrival of a creative thunderbolt, *begin with the second or third paragraph. Then* go back and write the lead. It'll probably be a better lead, actually, because you'll have had time to see how the content has developed and you'll now be able to creatively preview it.
- **Instead of Sitting There Bleeding onto the Keyboard Trying to Figure Out What to Say, Write Yourself a Memo about What You Want Yourself to Say**. For example, if you are assigned to write a major report, *don't start writing it.* Instead, assume the guise of your own editor and write a set of instructions to yourself. ("Open with an anecdote showing how e-mail miscommunication has resulted in a major account blowing up for us, and then move onto figures from the studies I've collected showing how this is a near-universal problem. For example, in the study from the University of Toronto . . .") If you follow this approach, three things will happen: (1) you'll take a lot of pressure off yourself, because giving instructions is a lot easier than actually doing the task, (2) after some tinkering, you'll come up with a logically ordered outline of the

piece when you write the memo, and (3) you'll probably find that your "examples" are well written and with a little revision you can just drop them into your draft.

- **Start with *Anything*, but Start *Now*.** Once you've started, *you become a person who has started*. It's like no longer being a virgin; once you cross that boundary, you can't go back. It's much easier, psychologically, to motivate yourself to keep pecking away at a project once it's under way, even only symbolically under way. Do you have a major project due in two weeks? Overcome your instinct to put it off until the night before the due date by writing *one paragraph* today. Write a sentence if you can't manage a paragraph. If you're really stuck, create a blank folder for the project. Anything! Having accomplished at least *something* today, you're facing a much less onerous task tomorrow because you'll be *continuing* the work, and not *starting* it. And don't be too fussy about what you write. You can always go back and edit it later. To paraphrase Churchill, insisting on perfection in your prose is a prescription for paralysis. Moreover, a day's thought and perspective on even the roughest of rough drafts can produce some pretty exciting insights into how the piece can be developed.

Chapter 2

_____

Use Proper Paragraphing to Grab Your Readers by the Nose and Lead Them through Your Piece (And Make Them *Like* Being Led)

You now know how to properly plan and begin a writing project. The first and most important major refinement we'll add to that foundation is the use of coherent paragraphing. A few simple tricks with paragraph construction will dramatically improve the clarity and flow of your prose—instantly. Professional writers have learned how to present the information in logical chunks and use a rhythm and structure that draws the reader through the piece. Here's how you can do that, too.

STEP 1: TRANSLATE YOUR OUTLINE INTO PARAGRAPHS

The outline encapsulates the basic thrust of each section of the piece, and the paragraphs express the individual thoughts in the basic thrust. So just use your judgment about when to make new paragraphs as you go through each in the outline section.

But how do you know when to change paragraphs? Make a new paragraph when:

- You change thoughts. Directly above I had two thoughts: The first was that you can use your judgment when writing at the paragraph level, and the second was a question leading into the discussion of how you know when to change paragraphs. I made them separate paragraphs to keep the sharpness of ideas clear.
- You introduce a quote. Generally, when you quote someone, it starts a new paragraph.
- Your paragraph gets too long. Paragraphs provide a place for the reader to take a mental breath. If the paragraph becomes too ponderous, you'll lose the reader's attention. When that happens, you need to change thoughts (even slightly) in order to justify a new paragraph. "Another reason I support this measure . . ." is an example of an easy way to break a long paragraph.

For more on how long a paragraph should be, see Step 5.

STEP 2: USE TOPIC SENTENCES FOR EACH IDEA; EACH IDEA = ONE PARAGRAPH

The topic sentence is the main thought to be expressed in the paragraph. Everything in the paragraph expands on the main thought.

Topic sentences typically come at the beginning of the paragraph. You can occasionally construct a paragraph that has the topic sentence at the end, but that's a device used for effect and is not a good idea for common practice.

STEP 3: MAKE ALL THE MATERIAL IN EACH PARAGRAPH SUPPORT THE TOPIC SENTENCE

The entire content of the paragraph must be congruent with the topic sentence. In other words, make the topic sentence a guide to what's coming in the rest of the paragraph and don't change subjects until you've finished that part of the discussion. That's what the phrase "support the topic sentence" means.

In journalism, we also instruct writers and reporters to "support the lead." That means that the writer should ensure that everything in the opening (see Chapter 1, Steps 3 and 4) is dealt with in the article and nothing *not* indicated in the opening is interjected. Supporting the topic sentence is the next logical step in that process. Simply by supporting the lead and supporting each topic sentence—a fairly easy practice once you are aware of the concept—you can dramatically improve the flow and clarity of your writing.

STEP 4: USE TRANSITIONS TO CONNECT ONE PARAGRAPH TO ANOTHER AND LEAD THE READER THROUGH YOUR MAIN POINTS

Graceful transitions ease the jarring jump between paragraphs. By mechanically connecting the paragraph above to the one that follows, you ensure a sense of flow that leads your reader through your piece point-by-point-by-point.

Transitions are a common device used by professional writers, who sometimes use the trick unconsciously, but when they are stuck, they mechanically wedge in transitions to keep the writing moving.

Here are some types of transitions you can use:

> *An echo transition. Pick up a word or idea from the paragraph above. Sometimes you can repeat a specific word:*

> *. . . timed for maximum **impact.***
> *The **impact** could be particularly devastating for the . . .*

> *A transition that shows contrast.*

> *. . . and they believe cell phones have no place in the office.*
> *That view is **far from universal**, however.*

> *A transition that shows agreement.*

> *. . . which the head of the bank contends will drive business away.*
> *The chairman of the local chamber of commerce **concurs.***

> *A transition that demonstrates a time linkage.*

> *. . . we rode out to the site of the accident.*
> *An **hour after we arrived**, it became obvious that the puzzle would not be solved any time soon.*
> *(This is sometimes known as the "meanwhile, back at the ranch" transition.)*

> *A transition that questions an element of the paragraph above.*

> *. . . spent over a million dollars on a lavish public relations campaign.*
> *But **was it worth it?** Initial figures were disappointing.*

There are two terrific benefits to using transitions to link your paragraphs:

1. Transitions are the ring and chain that allow you to pull your reader, nose-wise, through your assertions and arguments. Each new thought has a logical connection to the one before. Remember, readers *like* to be led. Paragraphs that seem offtrack are an irritant to the reader—and readers are fickle. They lose interest quickly and ruthlessly.
2. The effort to insert transitions troubleshoots the organization of your piece. If you can't, for the life of you, dream up some logical connection between a paragraph and the paragraph that follows, there is *something wrong with your organization*. It's time to reshuffle the order in order to make the piece cohesive.

STEP 5: ELIMINATE ANY ROGUE PARAGRAPHS THAT INTERRUPT THE FLOW

The best way to appreciate transitions is to see what happens without them—where there is a "rogue paragraph" that comes out of nowhere.

Note how the example that follows throws you offtrack momentarily because there is no immediate connection between the last sentence of the top paragraph and the first sentence of the bottom paragraph.

> *. . . importance of getting out the vote in the third district.*
>   *Marge Davis was appointed ward leader three months ago. She is a long-time union activist, and will now be in charge of a drive to whip up the vote.*

If the topic of the paragraph is completely out of line with the flow of the piece, you need to eliminate or move the paragraph. But usually, if the writing is basically coherent, the problem is in the transition, not the content, and the fix is easy. Use a transition to **connect top and bottom**.

> *. . . importance of getting out the vote in the third district.*
>   *The drive will be spearheaded by longtime union activist Marge Davis, who was appointed ward leader . . .*

By referencing "the drive," the writer keeps the main point in focus and moves on to the next subject in a logical fashion.

STEP 6: EMPLOY PARAGRAPH LENGTH THAT IS APPROPRIATE TO THE PIECE

Appropriate length largely depends upon the nature of the work. If you are writing a scholarly paper or a book review in an intellectual journal, your paragraphs can trend six, seven, eight sentences, or longer. You don't want to use a lot of short paragraphs in a piece such as that because the idea is to show you are delving deeply into each thought expressed.

On the other end of the scale, a newspaper article generally uses paragraphs not much longer than three sentences, and often a hard-news article will have many one-sentence paragraphs, especially when quotes are used. There's a reason: The purpose of a news report is to edit down information to the bare essentials and impart it quickly.

What you're reading now is written mostly in short paragraphs. That structure reinforces the basic idea of the book: useful information delivered rapidly. Also, the nature of this book—separate entries about wide-ranging instructions—compels me to change thoughts frequently.

STEP 7: PUNCH UP YOUR WRITING WITH ONE-SENTENCE PARAGRAPHS (SPARINGLY) FOR EMPHASIS

In the type of writing I'm doing here, I sometimes use one-sentence paragraphs, which focus the reader and propel the narrative forward.

But be careful.

Use the one-sentence paragraph like a condiment, not the main dish. A string of one-sentence and/or very short paragraphs in something other than a news report appears disjointed and creates the inevitable impression that the writer is offering a superficial view. That said, the one-sentence paragraph serves its purpose, as it did earlier, when I wrote "But be careful" with the intent of dangling a punchy line that would attract your interest and lead you to see that I am emphasizing the thought.

STEP 8: BEGIN SOME PARAGRAPHS WITH A QUESTION TO REVIVE YOUR READER'S ATTENTION

We are trained to respond to questions. Years of schooling have hard-wired us to spring to alertness when we are asked something, and the rules of social interaction demand that we not ignore questions. Asking questions is also a way we demonstrate interest in another person, so we are attuned to using them in both directions of conversation flow.

As a writer, you can exploit these tendencies by using questions to figuratively grab the readers by the lapels and yank them back into the narrative.

You can pose a question in the first or second sentence of the paragraph. The first-sentence question is direct and focuses attention on the flow of the previous paragraphs:

Who is to blame? There has been continual finger-pointing, but . . .

Posing a question in the second or third sentence is an elegant way to firm up interest in the topic sentence. Chris Harper, now a professor at Temple University in Philadelphia, employed this technique when writing for ABC correspondent Lynn Sherr. Note how the question focuses your attention in this segment of a piece about environmental contamination:

The discoveries here in Florida are not isolated. Similar bizarre changes have been found in animals throughout the world—panthers, eagles, even bats. What's causing this? Scientists aren't exactly certain, but they believe it may be a previously unknown effect of chemical substances we thought we'd cleaned up.

You can overdo this technique, of course, so limit your paragraph questions to perhaps one or two per article or report.

STEP 9: USE PROPER PARAGRAPH FORM TO INTRODUCE QUOTATIONS, ADDING LIFE AND HUMANITY TO YOUR WORK

Good quotes make a piece come alive. You can use quotes in almost any type of writing to lend authenticity, add interest, and draw the reader into a scene in the theater of the mind.

The use of quotes to tell a story is fully covered in Chapter 8, Steps 3 and 4, but it's important to address part of the subject here because quotes are an essential part of paragraphing, and in turn, proper paragraph structure is needed to best frame the quote.

Here is how you properly employ quotes.

Quotes are words written or spoken by another and are indicated by "quotation marks."

You don't have to use the full quote, and in fact it's usually advisable not to. You can paraphrase the dull parts, and put the interesting parts—ones that show color or firsthand knowledge—in direct quotes.

Johnson noted that the value of the stock declined by more than half in the last quarter, a drop he said "came out of the blue and just hit me like a sucker punch to the back of the head."

There's no point in quoting plain fact such as the stock decline. You can simply state that on your own (if you know the facts) or attribute in a paraphrase to the speaker. The "sucker punch" remark, though, is colorful and adds life to the piece so you want to use a direct quote.

Put the attribution (who said the statement) at the end of a quote, or in the case of a long quote, after the first sentence in the paragraph.

> *"It's touch-and-go whether we can come back from this," Johnson said. "It means that all our collateral for borrowing is gone, and because every company runs on credit . . ."*

(There is an exception to this rule involving changing speakers, and the exception is covered later in the chapter.)

You can use "says" in the attribution, which adds some present-tense liveliness to the quote, but in general it's best to stick to past tense. What someone said yesterday and what she "says" today may be different, so be careful.

There are three main paragraphing considerations when using quotes.

First, a quote should almost *always have its own paragraph*. In other words, make a new paragraph when introducing a quote. There are stylistic exceptions to this rule, but they are not worth noting.

Second, a long *series of quotes from the same person can be made into separate paragraphs*—a good idea if several topics are covered. Change paragraphs in the quote just like you would change them in any material—every time a new thought is introduced. If the quote continues from one paragraph to the next, don't put a quotation mark at the end of the first paragraph, but do put one at the beginning of the second.

> *"Unfortunately, this will result in massive layoffs."*
> *"No one thinks this is an easy situation, but we have to think about the long-term as well as the immediate crisis," Johnson said.*

The open quotation mark is a visual cue that the same person is still speaking.

Third, if you have a series of quotes from different speakers, put them in separate paragraphs and *put the attribution first when you change speakers.* Use a transition when indicating the attribution.

> *"The economy will undoubtedly recover within a month or two," said Harvard's John Smith.*

But Yale's Mary Johnson predicts the downturn will last into the new year. "Look, this is a crisis that deeply affects manufacturing," Johnson says, "and manufacturing is always the slowest sector to recover."

(Note that I used "says." In this case, use of the present tense to liven up the conversation—make it happen in real time, so to speak—is acceptable because it's a long-term observation made by Johnson, and not something pinned at a particular point in time.)

STEP 10: ELIMINATE THE AMATEUR'S TYPICAL REPETITIVE HABITS: "I TOLD YOU SO"–TYPE TAGGING AT THE END OF A PARAGRAPH AND REPEATING MATERIAL ALREADY STATED IN OTHER PARAGRAPHS

Never do this:

We don't seem to be learning from our mistakes. Four years after losing an election badly because we had no real ground game to speak of, we are five points behind and have no viable mechanism to get people to the polls in three weeks. The opposition has buses, a layered system of ward and block leaders, and will be monitoring each polling station to see who hasn't shown up by six o'clock and contact them. We have none of that. This shows that we haven't learned from the past.

Everything was fine up until the writer felt compelled to tag the paragraph with an unnecessary and redundant "I told you so" in the last sentence. Make your points, give examples, and then move on. Having to indicate "I told you so" actually weakens your case; the facts and arguments should speak for themselves.

Chapter 3

Employ Muscular, Accurate Words to Do Your Heavy Lifting

I'm sure you've noticed how some writing seems vague, leaden, and lethargic. But professional writing comes alive on the page—even when the subject is not particularly compelling. It doesn't happen by accident. Experienced writers choose words carefully, seeking maximum impact. Here's how you can use the strong word, the accurate word, and the word that makes your writing ring with energy and authenticity.

STEP 1: MAKE VERBS DO THE WORK

The human mind craves action. Action is the key ingredient in entertainment; we like movement, along with stories, and dialogue that engages us in the interaction between characters.

Movement is the spice provided by *verbs,* words that *communicate action.* There are two basic ways verbs can make your writing captivating ...

By adding action to a static event:

Instead of: *Bob was very angry after Sharon accused him of doing a bad job on the meeting.*

Use action writing packed with strong verbs: *Bob pounded the table and snarled at Sharon, denouncing her claim that he had bungled the meeting.*

By using exactly the right verb to add power and precision:

Instead of: *Wiped out*
Use a more colorful and specific verb: *Obliterated*

Instead of: *He said it was wrong*
Use: *He denounced it*

Generally, the fewer words you use to make a statement of action, the more powerful the action will be. This is especially true of extraneous words like "very" or "really." For example, I once coached a journalist who wrote:

The witness was really confused by the question.

I asked him how he could make "really confused" stronger. I was hoping for an answer such as "bewildered," which pares down the phrase and uses a more punchy and specific word. His suggestion was, "really, really confused."
No. Please, no.

STEP 2: REMEMBER THAT THE BEST ADVERB IS OFTEN NO ADVERB

An adverb is a word that modifies a verb. (The origin of the word is a Latin phrase that means "added word.") An adverb generally has "ly" at the end: "brightly," "hopefully," "defiantly," "brilliantly," and others. Other words that qualify verbs include "seldom," "often," "very," and the unfortunate "really."
The problem with adverbs and other words that modify verbs is that they often are used to prop up a weak verb or to provide a vague description of what should really be *shown* instead of *described*.

The honorary degree recipient wittily told everyone that he was a college dropout.

Almost any verb phrase would be better than "told everyone." But a larger issue is that the adverb "wittily" is used as a secondhand relay of what happened. In this case, the adverb was the crutch that saved the writer from the hard but rewarding work of crafting a scene. (There's more on scenes throughout Chapter 8.)
Rewrite the sentence with specifics and the action that *shows* the wit, not tells about it:

Safire said that he entered as a freshman decades ago and received his honorary doctorate today, noting that, "there's hope for even the slowest learner."

You don't have to banish adverbs, but eliminate them when possible. In particular, edit out adverbs or other verb modifiers that are unnecessary, prop up a weak verb, or are used as a lazy way to tell instead of show.

STEP 3: USE VIVID ADJECTIVES

Adjectives, words that describe, create images in the theater of the mind, the place where the code of writing is translated into intellectual meaning. Weak adjectives are worse than no adjectives at all because they dilute meaning and, in addition, make the writing tedious.

Invest some time in picking the right adjective. For example, consider how unappealing this entry would have been if it were titled, "Use Good Adjectives." Or how repulsive it would have been had I titled it, "Use Really, Really Good Adjectives." "Vivid," in my mind, was the strongest modifier because it portrayed exactly what I wanted to say—producing powerful, lifelike images. The origin of the word, in fact, comes from the Latin *vivere*, which means "to live." (Other words from *vivere* include "vivacious," "revive," and "viable." Knowing one root unlocks the meanings of many more words; more to come on this in Chapter 3, Step 7.)

Using the perfect adjectives to describe what the reader should be sensing in the theater of the mind adds a lifelike and compelling aspect to your writing. And don't limit yourself to the obvious: Describe, perhaps, the lighting, the mood, the demeanor of people in your paragraph, the smell of the room, the noise in the hallway.

George Orwell, the author primarily known for the book *1984*, was a brilliant essayist and could summon up meaningful adjectives as well as any writer who ever lived.

Bask in the brilliance of the first two paragraphs from his piece "A Hanging."

It was in Burma, a sodden morning of the rains. A sickly light, like yellow tinfoil, was slanting over the high walls into the jail yard. We were waiting outside the condemned cells, a row of sheds fronted with double bars, like small animal cages. Each cell measured about ten feet by ten and was quite bare within except for a plank bed and a pot of drinking water. In some of them brown silent men were squatting at the inner bars, with their blankets draped round them. These were the condemned men, due to be hanged within the next week or two.

One prisoner had been brought out of his cell. He was a Hindu, a puny wisp of a man, with a shaven head and vague liquid eyes. He had a thick, sprouting moustache, absurdly too big for his body, rather like the moustache of a comic man on the films. Six tall Indian warders were guarding him and getting him ready for the gallows. Two of them stood by with rifles and fixed bayonets, while the others handcuffed him, passed a chain through his handcuffs and fixed it to their belts, and lashed his arms tight to his sides. They crowded very close about him, with their hands always on him in a careful, caressing grip, as though all the while feeling him to make sure he was there. It was like men handling a fish which is still alive and may jump back into the water. But he stood quite unresisting, yielding his arms limply to the ropes, as though he hardly noticed what was happening.[1]

"Sickly light," "brown, silent men," "thick, sprouting mustache," "vague, liquid eyes"—all are constructions using sharp, gloriously perfect adjectives that add meaning and immediacy to the piece. (The entire essay is reprinted in Chapter 11, along with my commentary on the construction and mechanics of the piece.)

Follow Orwell's strategy. Put some thought into your adjective choices. Avoid mundane, bland, and vague adjectives. Find the precisely perfect adjective to make your writing sing.

If no word comes immediately to mind, use a thesaurus, online references, or the synonym finder on your word processing program to serve up a menu of options. Don't overdo it with obscure adjectives; sometimes the only word for "red" is "red." Unless it's the color of blood . . . then it's "scarlet."

STEP 4: CHOOSE THE RIGHT POWER WORD

Whether it's a noun, verb, or adjective, be sure to pick the right word—the word that is both *precise in meaning* and *forceful*. Remember that a forceful word is not necessarily complex or obscure (it is often just the opposite), and the goal of using a more sophisticated vocabulary is not to impress. Having said that, you *will* impress readers if you use a refined vocabulary that propels your writing by employing exactly the right word at the right time.

Notice the difference in these sentences.

We need to get rid of the hostile attitude that is all around in this company.
We need to eradicate the hostile attitude that pervades this company.

"Eradicate" is clearly the more powerful word, and closer in meaning to what I want to say that the pedestrian "get rid of." ("Pedestrian" is a fine power word, too, indicating something common that just plods along.) "Eradicate" is from the Latin word meaning "root" (think "radish" and hold that thought until Step 7) and means "rip out by the roots."

"Pervade" means spread throughout all the parts of something, another spin-off of Latin from two words meaning "go throughout." It's a better choice than "is all around" because "pervade" implies that the culture has spread everywhere, not just existed from day one in a few pockets. If the writer really felt the hostile attitude was pernicious (a good word, by the way), there are even stronger words that can be deployed. How about "has metastasized within," which alludes to a cancer that has spread?

Do you see the strategy? The *right word*, the most *powerful word*, used at the *right time*.

Compare these sentences. If you're curious, look up the origin of the words and check on the nuances of their meanings.

Weak: *He was really interested in the singer's performance.*
Strong: *He was captivated by the singer's performance,* or *He was transfixed by the singer's performance.*

Weak: *The politician's behavior was not very mature.*
Strong: *The politician's behavior was infantile.*

Weak: *His master's degree moved him into a different, higher type of group of executives.*
Strong: *His master's degree elevated him to a new echelon among the executives.*

Weak: *The loss of his job made him very sad.*
Strong: *The loss of his job devastated him.*

Weak: *The waiter has a really conceited and stuck-up attitude and shows it when he deals with people.*
Strong: *The waiter demonstrates his contempt for the customers through his supercilious attitude.* (I can't help myself … you *need* to see the story behind this word now. It involves eyebrows. How can you resist? Check out Step 7.)

STEP 5: BE CERTAIN NOT TO MIX UP SIMILAR-SOUNDING WORDS THAT HAVE DIFFERENT MEANINGS

I recently came across a brochure for public relations services where the writer extolled his value and intellect, at one point gushing:

My solution to your problems is simplistic!

He meant "simple," of course. "Simplistic" means oversimplified to the point of being misleading or ignoring significant details.

There is no failsafe way to avoid confusing similar-sounding words, but I have a two-part strategy that I believe is as good as any and better than most.

- Learn the most commonly confused words and *develop a trick* to remember the proper usages.
- Learn to *identify the warning signs* of a word that may sound like one word but have a different meaning or connotation ("connotation" means a feeling that a word creates, not its strict definition).

Commonly Confused Words

I could fill this entire book with lists of confused words. I won't, because that's something you can easily find on the Web, and in addition, in your business or special area of writing you may deal with specific troublesome words that I cannot anticipate.

But for discussion, here are the top confused word pairs (in my estimation) that I see interchanged in standard writing. (I am not including "its/it's" or "your/you're" because they are covered more appropriately in Chapter 5, which deals with grammar and apostrophe usage.) I'll then propose a way you can keep them straight in your head.

Affect:	An action word meaning "to have an impact on." "This new law will affect my decision."
Effect:	A noun referring to a change that resulted because of an action. "The effect of the new law has been disastrous."
Accept:	Agree to take.
Except:	Not include.
Infer:	Deduce, figure out.
Imply:	Hint.
Disinterested:	Impartial, with no conflict of interest in the outcome, such as a "disinterested third party."
Uninterested:	Not caring.
Principle:	Something that you believe in or stand for.
Principal:	A person with an important role, such as the principal of a school or the principal clarinetist of the New York Philharmonic.
Formerly:	Before.
Formally:	Officially or through appropriate channels.

Ensure:	To make certain.
Insure:	To buy a policy that protects against loss.

Compliment:	A word or two of praise.
Complement:	Something that adds to or improves something else, such as a tie that "complements" the color of a suit jacket.

Aid:	A *thing* that is provided to help, such as "monetary aid to destitute families."
Aide:	A *person* who acts as an assistant.

Discrete:	Separate.
Discreet:	Understated, showing caution in words and actions.

Comprise:	The difference between "comprise" and "compose" can be tricky and even experienced editors and grammarians will quibble about the nuances. But in general, you are always safe if you use "comprise" to mean "consists of." A memory trick is this sentence: "The whole comprises the parts." You can substitute any "whole" for any parts and use the word correctly. For example: "New Jersey comprises 21 counties."
Compose:	Compose means made up from different parts. In other words, "The parts compose the whole." "New Jersey is composed of 21 counties."

But How Do You Remember the Differences?

One way is to develop a memory trick to aid recall, a device defined as a mnemonic. (The "m" is silent; it's pronounced neh-MONN-ick.) A mnemonic can be a word or rhyme—whatever works for you. Those of us among the ranks of the mechanically disinclined, for example, have to recite the mnemonic "lefty loosy righty tighty" every time we pick up a screwdriver.

A common mnemonic to remember the distinction between principle and principal is "the principal of your school is your pal." This device emphasizes that the principal is a person, rather than an ideal, because only a person can be a pal. And, of course, the mnemonic cues you to the spelling of "pal" in the usage.

Another: The word "affect" is an action word, while "effect" is not. (Note: Just to confuse things, there is a correct usage of the word "effect" as a verb when you mean "to bring about," but worry about that relatively rare usage sometime in the future.) The scheme is simple: *The "A" in "affect" stands for action.*

The best mnemonic for me is one that I create in the bizarre little universe of my own mind. I used to have a tendency to mix up "complement" and "compliment." I invented the memory device when you want to use complement to mean "add something extra," use the "e" for "extra."

I also tended to mix up "discreet" and "discrete." I solved this by reminding myself that in the version of the word that means "separate" the Es are separate from each other.

The human brain is disposed to respond to associations (much more so than to rote memorization), so don't be reluctant to invent silly comparisons to help you remember. The sillier the better, in fact. Memory guru Harry Lorayne, who was popular on television shows in the 1960s and 1970s, would sometimes memorize the names of the entire studio audience—sometimes hundreds of people. How? By picturing the person in a situation or image that jogged his memory. If a woman was named "Beth," for example, he might picture her sitting in a bath.

Use *whatever works for you.* Be creative. An Internet memory guru who identifies himself only as Douglas provided this hint for remembering that Sofia is the capital of Bulgaria: Picture a bull named Gary—it helps if he is wearing a sweatshirt with "Gary" emblazoned on it—relaxing on a sofa. A "bull named Gary" relaxing in a sofa is a hard image to get out of your mind . . . as (now) is the fact the Sofia is the capital of Bull-Gary-Uh.

What about Words That Sound Similar but You Don't or Can't Remember the Meanings?

You'll have to look them up. But realistically, you can't look up every word you use. You will need a trigger to alert you that the word you plan to employ might not mean what you think.

To accomplish this, be on the alert for words that have these characteristics:

1. *They have some component such as "istic" or "ism."* These types of components are called "adjective suffixes" or "noun suffixes" and exist to form a descriptive word based on a noun. Meanings, however, are often changed considerably in the process. Confusion between "simple" and "simplistic" is a good example. So is "social" and "socialism." The reason is that word usages evolve over time via their suffixes. The word "terrific," for example, 150 years ago used to have the more literal meaning of "inspiring terror."

2. *They share a common sound or component with another word that seems like it means the same thing or something similar.* For instance,

don't mix up the words "ostracize" and "criticize." The similar sound of the words should be enough to tip you off that you need to look them up because it is *highly unlikely there would be a need for two similar-sounding words that mean the same thing.* "Criticize" means to find fault in a judgmental way. It is actually derived from a Latin word meaning "judge." "Ostracize" means to shun or cast out someone and it has a totally different origin—coming from a Greek word meaning (loosely) "tile," the surface on which citizens of Athens would write the name of someone they considered deserving of a ten-year banishment.

Note: There are many words that *while not confused directly with similar words* are nonetheless *used incorrectly.* We address some of them in the next entry.

STEP 6: MAKE SURE YOU KNOW WHAT WORDS *REALLY* MEAN

"Fulsome" means overblown to the point of being offensive. Using it to convey a positive meaning is simply wrong.

OK, get out your pencils. What does "notoriety" mean? "Obtuse?" "Hopefully?" "Literally?"

"Notoriety" means the state of being notorious, and "notorious" means known for some bad quality or predilection toward evil.

Both words are commonly misused by decidedly common communicators and instantly betray a lack of sophistication. Worse, using such words incorrectly gives the impression that you are intellectually underpowered but trying to impress people with your vocabulary—a double whammy.

I know this answer seems simplistic (and now, thanks to Step 5, we both know what I mean), but the answer to this problem is to look words up—all the time, if you have any suspicion that there might be nuances of their use with which you're unfamiliar. A dictionary is as close as your smartphone. I look up words frequently, and often catch myself in errors or misconceptions.

For example, recently I almost referred to someone's argument as "obtuse," thinking the word meant only "poorly reasoned." In a way it does, because one meaning is "hard to understand," but the definition offered in most dictionaries also means "slow to understand"—basically, "stupid." I didn't intend to call the person or the argument stupid, so I'm glad I looked it up.

There are also mutated usages of common words that are incorrect. Don't misuse "hopefully." It's an adverb meaning to do something with hope, such as, "he looked at the letter hopefully." It doesn't mean "it is to be hoped."

Don't write something like "he literally wiped the floor with the candidate who ran against him," unless, of course, the person in question actually physically used the person to wipe the floor. You don't mean "literally." You mean "figuratively."

STEP 7: EXPAND YOUR VOCABULARY BY UNDERSTANDING THE STORIES BEHIND WORDS

Did you know the meaning of the word "supercilious," which was used as an example in Step 4? It means acting as though you believe yourself to be superior, a word we might apply to someone who gives us a disdainful facial expression, such as peering down from beneath raised eyebrows. Will you remember the definition I just gave you? *Yes*, because it means "eyebrow!" It's from two Latin words, *super*, which means "above," and *cilium*, which means "eyelid."

The stories behind words are terrific mnemonic devices to help you remember them. Also, once you know one root, the knowledge can help you figure out words with similar origins.

For example, a useful Latin word to know is *sid*, which also has the variant *sed*. (Latin words sometimes change spelling according to their usage in a sentence.) It means "sit," and in fact the English word was formed as sort of a melding of the two.

Sid and *sed* unlock many word meanings. "Sedate" is someone who sits a lot. "Sedative" is something that compels you to sit or lie down. A "dissident" is someone who sits apart, with the word dating back to religious splinter groups who sat apart from others during worship.

You may want to become friends with the word "insidious," meaning something that is gradual, sneaky, not easily noticed and very harmful, such as "the insidious spread of high blood pressure in America." It also can refer to a plot that is meant to trap someone after luring them in.

It's an enormously versatile and useful word, but will you remember it? Yes, you will. Watch me, now . . .

"Insidious" comes from the Latin *sid*. Roman soldiers would "wait sitting down"—concealed, in other words—and then suddenly spring into ambush. *Isidere* came to mean "lie in wait for," and it evolved in to the present-day English. So, an insidious problem is one that will ambush you from concealment, just like the crouching Roman soldiers.

Now, will you ever forget the meaning of "insidious"? Not a chance. *Try* to forget it now that you know the story. Just *try*.

I know this is something of a radical approach to expanding your vocabulary . . . and by the way, did I mention where "radical" comes from? It's from the Latin *radix*, which is easy to remember because it's basically the same as "radish," and means "root." It usually means relating to the fundamental nature of something, and a radical is someone who wants to change the root aspects of, say, a political system. As mentioned before, to "eradicate" means to pull out all the way to the roots.

But I digress. Learning the stories and the interlocking relationships among words is a radical approach, but it not only exposes you to more words but makes learning, deciphering, and remembering them easier and, I daresay, fun. Almost any reputable dictionary, online or in print, has a section on the word's "etymology," or origin. It doesn't take long to become very well versed in word origins, and before long you can become like me, endlessly explaining these fascinating stories to people as they back away nervously.

STEP 8: EDIT OUT VAGUE WORD MEANINGS AND UNCLEAR REFERENCES, PARTICULARLY IN YOUR OPENING SENTENCES

Here is a real head-scratcher from an e-mail report I received recently:

I am considering the approach that his company offered. The proposal arrived yesterday, and there is a difference in quality between it and the competitor's.

What? Was the quality better or worse? Over the next ten meandering paragraphs, he didn't tell me—assuming, for some reason, I knew about proposals I had not seen.

Readers can only perceive what you put on paper; they cannot read your mind. You need to be crystal clear in your meanings. Before you send an e-mail, mail a letter, or give an editor your manuscript, read it over and ask yourself whether someone NOT living inside your head and sharing your thoughts will understand what you are getting at.

I wish the person who wrote that e-mail had told me, simply, what was on his mind—clarifying near the beginning of the report exactly what he was getting at—the "one central idea" concept we examined in Chapter 1, Step 3.

Writing that opens in a vague, unclear way rarely recovers.

Make no mistake, writing a good opening is hard work. Experienced newspaper reporters and editors, for example, always sweat over their "leads," the opening that, when used in the context of news reporting, usually contains the top developments about the *who, what, where, when,* and sometimes *why,* and also sets the agenda for the rest of the story. If the lead is fuzzy, the reader becomes confused, perhaps irritated, and quickly loses interest. Aside from that, a story with a bad lead ultimately fails in its mission: to give the reader a clear picture of what's happening in the world.

You don't always have to put the *who, what, where, when,* and *why*— what journalists sometimes call the "five Ws"—in the opening. You can, as we've discussed, open with an indirect lead, a story that hooks the reader and illustrates what's coming. That's fine—as long as the ultimate purpose is clear near the top of whatever it is you are writing.

Let's talk about hard and soft leads and the structure of the stories that follow the leads in the context of journalism for a moment. There are two basic structures for journalistic writing, and now you know both of them. One is designed for hard-news reporting, and puts the information up top. That's the same concept as a direct lead you would use for any type of writing, but puts more emphasis on the five Ws. Information is then imparted in descending order of importance. This format actually is an artifact of reporting during the Civil War, when information was sent over a telegraph. Telegraph time was expensive and the transmission was sometimes cut arbitrarily, so the important information had to be up top.

The other type of journalistic lead is called the "feature" lead. It's an indirect lead that begins with a compelling story, then introduces the main theme, continues with examples and quotes, and ends with a quote or story that usually relates back to the premise—the feature structure.

In actuality, most writing of any type follows either one or the other structure. A memo or report can begin with a statement of the main point, or it might open with an example that illustrates the issue and continues with examples and details. Often, a memo or report is a hybrid of the two; it may open with hard information, but generally contains a summary or call to action at the end, rather than simply revealing less-important details in diminishing order of importance.

The purpose of this section is not to train you in writing newspaper leads, although many readers may be using the book to fortify journalism skills.

Rather, it's to show you how a bad opening puts the rest of the piece not on the fairway but in the weeds, and how an improved lead can serve as a promising tee shot.

I'm going to show you bad leads, explain why they are bad, and show you how to fix them. Following are three actual leads from real stories I re-wrote when I was editor of a weekly international news publication. The reporters weren't bad writers, but in these cases they needed an extra set of eyes to focus on the actual meaning of the event and re-order the contents of the opening sentences. Remember, even if your goal is not journalistic writing, the lead is the most important part of any piece you compose and it has to be clear.

With that in mind, here is a confused and puzzling lead:

> *Michael Milken the long-penalized pioneer of junk bond investing, agreed to pay a $47-million settlement with the SEC this week. Milken's latest settlement, added to $1.1 billion in fines for his financial improprieties in the 1980s, brings his contentious relationship with the SEC to a tenuous close.*

There are several things wrong with this lead, the most serious being that the main idea is "buried." Milken's settlement apparently *put an end to his squabbling with the government*—that's the meat of the story. Also, the lead assumes that the reader knows about Milken and knows what the SEC is. At the time this story was written, Milken had been skirmishing with the law for decades, since the 1980s, in fact, so some readers would not have been familiar with his story.

Here's how I fixed it:

> *Michael Milken, the "junk bond king" who came to symbolize greed and financial recklessness throughout a long career involving risky and sometimes calamitous investments, last week agreed to pay $47 million in a settlement that appears to put an end to the government's string of actions against him.*
>
> *Milken's latest payment involves a civil lawsuit in which the Securities and Exchange Commission, the federal agency regulating stocks, charged him with violating . . .*

Here is a lead that tries to pack in too much information, and leaves the reader wondering what, exactly, the story is actually about.

> *Citing the results of its recent survey, Hong Kong-based Political & Economic Risk Consultancy (PERC) gave Asian nations a mixed grade on their efforts to curb economic corruption. The newly released PERC study reports that six of 11 Asian countries have witnessed increased rates of corruption. According to the study's polled executives, corruption has fallen significantly in South Korea and China. But other nations, most notably Indonesia and Japan, have been hard hit during the recent Asian economic meltdown.*

I fixed it by putting the *overall meaning* in plain English first, giving a snapshot of what happened, and then filling in the details.

> *A new survey of corruption in Asia shows mixed results, awarding high marks to China, South Korea, and Singapore but giving poor grades to Japan, Indonesia, and Thailand.*
>
> *The Hong-Kong based research firm Political & Economic Risk Consultancy (PERC) found that out of 11 Asian nations surveyed, six saw corruption decline while five witnessed an increase.*
>
> *[Effects of the economic meltdown are described later in the story, with examples from Japan.]*

Now, here's a lead that tries to provide background, which is good, but it puts the background *first*, confusing the reader. The actual news is buried at the end of the second paragraph.

> *Late last year, India's Supreme Court announced its decision to ban the practice of professional blood donation to the nation's blood banks. The decision led many Indians to fear a coming health crisis this spring. By enacting the ban, India's government hopes to cut off the supply of contaminated blood currently flooding the nation's healthcare system. Critics worry that the suddenness of the ban will lead to further problems, initiating a black market for professional blood donors.*

I fixed it by putting the real news first, in plain English, stressing what is happening *now* and why it's *important*. Then I provided the context, answering the question that would probably appear in the reader's mind after reading the opening paragraph.

> *Health officials in India worry that the recent decision by the nation's Supreme Court to ban purchase of blood from paid donors may prompt a health crisis this spring, when the ban is expected to lead to a short blood supply and an unregulated black market in paid donations.*
>
> *India's government issued the ban on paid donations—and on professional blood banks that pay for blood—in hopes of stanching the flow of infected blood that had flooded the country's health-care system. In a nation racked by poverty, the sale of blood is an attractive option, but one that frequently appeals to alcoholics and drug addicts. Some blood bank operators failed to screen the purchased blood for viruses and contaminants such as HIV and hepatitis.*
>
> *But if the supply dries up, critics say a black market . . .*

In sum: When you write anything, especially the beginning . . .

- Be sure your meanings are clear; ask yourself if someone else not living inside your head will understand exactly what you are referring to.
- Summarize the overall meaning in plain English first, then fill in details. You don't have to start with something that looks like a lead in a newspaper story about late-breaking developments, but you do have to have the central idea clearly presented somewhere in the first couple of paragraphs. If you start with a story or example for an indirect lead, be sure it links with your main point and then get to the main point quickly.
- Start with what's important to the reader.
- Layer context and detail so that the reader gets the full picture—but don't lead with detail.

STEP 9: REMOVE LOADED WORDS OR THOSE THAT CAN BE EASILY MISCONSTRUED

Certain words are ugly: "propaganda," "screed," "ignorant." You can't use them in a nice way. You can write "you apparently didn't know the policy involving use of the company flamethrower . . ." and make it seem polite. You cannot write "you are apparently ignorant of the policy . . ." and have it sound nice in any way.

If you firmly want to use one of these types of ugly words, believe you have justification, and predict that your writing will benefit from your bluntness and candid accuracy, go ahead.

But be wary of unintentionally inflaming a situation by using loaded words (loaded with implied meaning, usually bad) when you don't mean to suggest their full connotation. To return to the "igno-rant" example, I once was drawn into a full-scale verbal shooting war when serving on a committee considering a controversial issue, and someone sent me a letter claiming I was "ignorant of the past history" of the people involved in the issue in question.

I was doubly riled. First of all, there is no reason to write "past his-tory." History by its definition is past, so the writer needed to edit out a redundant word (I am teasing you with information about Step 10, by the way). More importantly, I resented being called "ignorant." In truth, I knew some, but not all, of the background, so technically the accusation was at least partly correct and I was the first person to admit I didn't have the whole story. But the author of the letter lost all my sympathy—and in fact recruited an enemy—because of the choice of a loaded word. I fired back a similarly misguided missile, she sent one back, though nowhere near as devilishly devastating as mine, and a lot of time and adrenaline was wasted.

I eventually crossed paths with the author of the letter and found that she was not particularly hostile, but not particularly possessed of verbal skills—or social skills, for that matter. She apparently did not realize the way the word "ignorant," while essentially accurate, would poison the tone of the communication.

So be on the lookout for loaded words. Ask yourself if the word is accurate, if it's really what you want to *say*, and also what you want to *imply*.

STEP 10: ELIMINATE UNNECESSARY OR REDUNDANT WORDS

Wordiness is insidious (see, I told you you'd remember that word): Without you realizing it, wordiness undermines the readability of your writing and undercuts your credibility at the same time.

Don't use a handful of words to express a thought that could better be encapsulated by one power word. Take out "pretty much does what we need done" and substitute "adequate." Pare down "really, really funny" into "hilarious." Whittle away at "extremely surprised, having no idea" until it becomes "astonished."

Too many words all saying the same thing—and saying it in a lame way—make writing tepid and lackluster.

Redundant words actually call attention to themselves, braying the fact that the user is an amateurish writer.

Some writers use redundant structure habitually, perhaps because they believe it seems precise, thoughtful, and lawyerly. I've actually seen the following:

> *The documents should be kept with the car or vehicle. (Huh? Why not just "vehicle?")*

> *Be careful how you dress at your job or place of employment. (Is anyone's job not their place of employment?)*

Unnecessary modifiers are among the most toxic redundancies because they are structurally incorrect:

- *Close proximity (proximity means being close)*
- *Past history (history is the past)*
- *Assemble together (assemble means to put or come together)*

- *True fact (a fact by definition is true)*
- *Free gift (a gift means something that's free)*
- *Absolutely certain (certain means that you know absolutely)*

I'll postpone until later (*did you catch my excess wordiness?—postpone means put off until later*) discussion of other errors in sentence construction and usage, but let me close this section by noting that editing out extraneous words is easy once you get into the habit of hunting them down when you proofread your work.

Chapter 4

Make Your Writing Come Alive with Vivid Style

You've learned how to make your writing organized, powerful, and accurate. Now you want to make it stand out. I'm sure you've noticed how some writing is especially moving, entertaining, and intriguing, qualities that are easy to recognize in a general way but not always easy to identify—to put your finger on something and say, "there, that's what gives this piece great style." But once you know what you're looking for, you can recognize many of those devices and appropriate them for your own writing. Here's how ...

STEP 1: CREATE POWERFUL IMAGES WITH FIGURATIVE WORDS AND PHRASES

Following is one of the greatest pieces of descriptive writing I've ever encountered. It's from a Pulitzer Prize–winning piece about the investigation of an airplane crash. Here is how reporter David Hanners described the wreckage:

> *The fates seem capricious in what is torn apart and what isn't when a large airplane crashes. Large pieces of metal dot the pasture, but between them lie tiny bits and pieces, indistinguishable now in their deformity.*
>
> *It is a fertile garden of disaster. Strands of writing lie here, a few rain-soaked playing cards lie there. A shredded Diet Pepsi can lies on the*

ground, while a few feet away, the door of the Westwind 2's cabin refrigera-
tor lies flattened—the row of small cans of tomato and orange juice that line
the shelf flattened neatly along with it.[1]

Figurative writing expands on the literal meaning of words to create an evocative mental image. There are different types of figurative writing that you no doubt confronted in high school, such as *metaphors, similes,* and *personification.*

We'll define those specific techniques later in this section, but at this point simply focus on the technique Hanners used (it's a metaphor, actually) and why it works so well.

Why is it so powerful?

- It *creates an image* in the mind. "Fertile garden of disaster" brings to mind a concrete, vivid scene.
- It uses *specific images that we all understand and can visualize.* Weak figurative language lacks this quality. For example, "it crashed with the force of 25 pounds of TNT" means little to me because I don't have any TNT around and don't know what 25 pounds of it would do, specifically, other than make a big mess. Better to say something like, "it crashed with enough force to pulverize a 10-foot boulder," or something similar. In this piece, the author consistently uses relatable images.
- It is *reinforced with authentic and arresting detail*—the playing cards, the flattened refrigerator, the shredded can, the scattered pieces "indistinguishable now in their deformity."
- It's *clever and compact*, drawing attention to its poetic use of language. And the figurative nature of the description is exponentially more brawny than an extended descriptive list of the debris or vague and pedestrian descriptions like the one I just used as a joke: "a big mess."

Look for opportunities to use creative interpretations of language to create a memorable image; use the four points listed here for guidance. Be careful because if you overdo it, the result can be self-conscious, obviously mechanical, or obscure. But take this risk. Remember that the four words "fertile garden of disaster" supplant an entire page of mundane description.

Sometimes you can riff on figurative images—take an image and run with it, letting it become comical— to great effect. Are you familiar with the Trivago Guy of the ubiquitous television commercials?

Slate writer Troy Patterson is masterful in his description of the Trivago Guy "a sallow avatar of middle-aged masculinity, a found object and a cult item, an accidental enigma."

Just look at this guy. The voice is deep with command, round with Shatner-
ian ham gravity, rich with a Peter Graves graininess. The eyes are beseeching

but confidently steady. The clothes have been woken up in. The man is seed-
ily creased, grayly stubbled, distractingly beltless. He may be looking for a
hotel after coming home at 3 a.m. to find that his wife changed the locks.
These unusual ads have been attracting baffled notice for a while, but now
is the season for big travel-industry ad buys, and the Trivago pitchman is,
unlike the blades of his rotary shaver, in heavy rotation.[2]

In sum: All the plain-fact description you can summon would not
match the power and accuracy of describing the Trivago Guy as someone who may be looking for a hotel room because his wife changed
the locks.

STEP 2: DRIVE YOUR POINT HOME WITH CREATIVE SIMILES, METAPHORS, AND PERSONIFICATION

A simile compares two things, usually by saying, in some fashion,
A is like *B*. A metaphor describes *A* by imagining or pretending it's
B. Personification portrays a non-human thing with human-like
qualities.

Simile:	*Bob is as crafty as a jungle cat.*
Metaphor:	*Bob is a prowling leopard, ready to pounce on anyone who shows a lack of loyalty.*
Personification:	*The lion crept forward diagonally, playing a slow and deadly game of chess with its prey.*

Figurative language adds interest and liveliness to writing and, if it's
cleverly enacted, draws attention to the point you want to make.
Compare:

> *She really doesn't seem to know that much about what is required to run a cam-*
> *paign. She more or less keeps it together, but could lose control at any minute.*

with

> *She has a thumbless grip on her campaign strategy.*

The metaphor says it all, with only 25 percent of the verbiage, and
it's funny and memorable.

Figurative language is powerful because it nudges the reader to view
something through a different lens, a fresh perspective. For example,
in *East of Eden*, John Steinbeck uses a vivid simile to create an intriguing vision of someone thinking slowly and carefully:

> *Kate inched over her own thoughts like a measuring worm.*

It's hard to top "fertile garden of disaster," but Shakespeare wrote what is arguably the world's most famous metaphor, describing life, in *As You Like It*, by re-imagining life as a seven-act play:

> All the world's a stage,
> And all the men and women merely players;
> They have their exits and their entrances,
> And one man in his time plays many parts,
> His acts being seven ages. At first, the infant,
> Mewling and puking in the nurse's arms.
> Then the whining schoolboy, with his satchel
> And shining morning face, creeping like snail
> Unwillingly to school. And then the lover,
> Sighing like furnace, with a woeful ballad
> Made to his mistress' eyebrow. Then a soldier,
> Full of strange oaths and bearded like the pard,
> Jealous in honor, sudden and quick in quarrel,
> Seeking the bubble reputation
> Even in the cannon's mouth. And then the justice,
> In fair round belly with good capon lined,
> With eyes severe and beard of formal cut,
> Full of wise saws and modern instances;
> And so he plays his part. The sixth age shifts
> Into the lean and slippered pantaloon,
> With spectacles on nose and pouch on side;
> His youthful hose, well saved, a world too wide
> For his shrunk shank, and his big manly voice,
> Turning again toward childish treble, pipes
> And whistles in his sound. Last scene of all,
> That ends this strange eventful history,
> Is second childishness and mere oblivion,
> Sans teeth, sans eyes, sans taste, sans everything.[3]

Shakespeare used another play metaphor when Macbeth contemplates the futility of life:

> Life's but a walking shadow, a poor player,
> That struts and frets his hour upon the stage,
> And then is heard no more. It is a tale
> Told by an idiot, full of sound and fury,
> Signifying nothing.[4]

Poet A. E. Housman uses some truly poetic personification, which makes sense because he is a poet, in "Loveliest of Trees, the Cherry Now."

Loveliest of trees, the cherry now
Is hung with bloom along the bough,
And stands about the woodland ride
Wearing white for Eastertide.[5]

Use figurative language in moderation. Too much is like a chef using everything in the spice rack to mix up a stew and cooking it all together with every bit of meat he can find in a hurry even roadkill he found while speeding down the information highway and ARE YOU GETTING THE POINT? Don't overdo.

Be especially careful of what's called a mixed metaphor, in which disparate points of comparison don't make sense.

This should be simple . . . it's not rocket surgery.

It's not rocket science or brain surgery, but there's no such thing as rocket surgery.

How about this metaphor?

I'm going to let it go. It's water over the bridge.

The common metaphor is *water under the bridge.* Or *water over the dam.* Either is fine, but water *over* the bridge describes a far different and much more serious issue.

STEP 3: ENGAGE THE READER WITH SPECIFICS—COLORS, SMELLS, DETAILS

In literal terms, writing engages only one of the human senses; you can only see the written word. But you can figuratively move your readers into a more realistic and evocative world by filling in more sensory information for them.

What did a fire scene smell like? What color uniform is the soldier wearing? Did the person giving the speech have to shout over protestors?

Don't skimp on details. Use *specifics.* Bland, vapid description removes the reader from the reality of the scene, essentially blurring the lens of the internal camera that's relaying the scene into the reader's head.

For example, don't write:

Jim Davis is a big former football player.

Instead:

> *Jim Davis is a 6'4," 250-pound former linebacker who played at the University of Alabama and regularly sports a collection of his alma mater's red-and-white neckties.*

One of the best examples of vivid writing that engages the reader with specifics is Edward R. Murrow's description of wartime London when he was reporting by radio. Murrow had only the power of the written word spoken over a microphone to propel the power of his reports. While he was occasionally able to include background noise, there were no pictures and no sophisticated sound effects available to fill in the sensory blanks. He was careful about composing description. Some of what he reported was ad-libbed, but much was carefully committed to paper before being read aloud.

Here is a classic example of his depiction of a blitzkrieg attack:

> *The fires up the river had turned the moon blood red. The smoke had drifted down till it formed a canopy over the Thames; the guns were working all around us, the bursts looking like fireflies in a southern summer night. . . . Huge pear-shaped bursts of flame would rise up into the smoke and disappear. The world was upside down. . . .*

And in this excerpt, note how Murrow invokes sight, sound, and smell:

> *There are no words to describe the thing that is happening. A row of automobiles, with stretchers racked on the roofs like skis, standing outside of bombed buildings. A man pinned under wreckage where a broken gas main sears his arms and face . . . But you can have little understanding of the life in London these days—the courage of the people, the flash and roar of the guns rolling down the streets . . . the stench of air-raid shelters in the poor districts. These things must be experienced to be understood.*[6]

STEP 4: TAKE ADVANTAGE OF ACCESSIBLE ALLITERATION

Alliteration means beginning two or more works with the same letter or sound, and it is a very successful stylistic device that adds dash to writing. In addition, there's no great trick to it. Anyone with a working knowledge of the alphabet and a thesaurus can employ this trick; it's accessible to everyone. The fact that I can label alliteration as "accessible" also gave me the opportunity to alliterate this section's heading.

Alliteration is one of many stylistic devices. The full range is beyond the scope of this work, but if you are interested I recommend Mark Forsyth's *The Elements of Eloquence: The Perfect Turn of Phrase.* (It has, of course, a cleverly alliterated and hence memorable title.) Forsyth advises:

> *Any phrase, so long as it alliterates, is memorable and will be believed even if it's a bunch of nonsense. . . .*
>
> *Nobody has ever thrown a baby out with the bathwater, nor is there anything particularly right about rain. Even when something does make a bit of sense, it's usually obvious why the comparison was picked. It takes two to tango, but it takes two to waltz as well. There are whole hogs, but why not pigs? Bright as a button. Cool as a cucumber. Dead as a doornail.*[7]

STEP 5: USE PRESENT TENSE WHEN APPROPRIATE

If doing so doesn't distort the factuality of the situation, you can use the present tense. Present tense imparts a feeling of immediacy, bringing the reader into the action, watching it unfold in real time.

In most cases, writing in the present tense usually involves not much more than using "says" instead of "said." You can also phrase action in the present tense: "He stalks into the room, and slams his notes on the lectern."

In the journalistic world, present tense is usually used for lighter, feature stories in print journalism, while past tense is employed for hard news in print. In broadcast, present tense is generally favored throughout because the whole impetus behind broadcast news is to tell the listener or viewer what is happening now.

The general rule of thumb is to use present tense (says) in less formal writing, usually when you are trying to tell a story or construct a narrative that draws the reader in. Use past tense for any occasion where it is important to pin actions in time. For example, "Shortly after the market results were announced, Mr. Murray said that layoffs appeared inevitable."

STEP 6: SPOTLIGHT IRONIES AND INCONGRUITIES

Suppose you are writing about a plane crash. Note how in Step 1 writer Hanners chose to illustrate the suddenness of the crash, and the devastating power with which it scrambled the lives of those aboard, by pointing out the incongruity between the open field where the crash took place and the presence of a refrigerator door that fell from the sky—complete with flattened cans of tomato and orange juice lining the shelves.

Here is what I think is the most impactful line of this section:

> *Nearby, partly stuck in the mud, a $50 bill flaps limply in the breeze.*
> *A page from a Jeppson pilot handbook has been charred and torn from its binding, but only a few feet away, a thick stack of computer printouts lies undamaged, still held together by a rubber band.*[8]

Consider how much more compact and powerful that line is that an extended thesis on how "the crash was sudden, it really, really messed up people's lives, it scattered stuff around, stuff you wouldn't expect to find so it was kind of jarring. . . ."

Irony has many definitions, but in writing it generally refers to a situation that is contrary to what you would expect, and so dramatically contrary that it points out the stark contrast and in the process makes a larger point.

For example, a depiction of sailors dying of thirst because they have no fresh water and are adrift in undrinkable salt seawater becomes compact and powerful in the hands of poet Samuel Taylor Coleridge, who points out the cruel irony of being thirsty in an ocean:

> *Water, water, every where,*
> *And all the boards did shrink;*
> *Water, water, every where,*
> *Nor any drop to drink.*[9]

STEP 7: EXPLOIT THE POWER OF THREES

For some unknown reason, expressions that have three parts are very powerful and memorable. This isn't my theory; it's an accepted truism among the writing community, especially speech-writers. Whether it is a function of some hard-wired aspect of the brain, a nuance related to the construction of the English language, or simply a pattern that registers because we are used to hearing, it is a question beyond my pay grade.

Regardless of the reason, the power of threes aids impact and memorability. Think of titles that have burned their way into your brain: "The Good, the Bad, the Ugly." Or famous lines from historical documents: "Life, liberty, and the pursuit of happiness."

Imagine how lifeless this speech would have been:

> *This nation, under God, shall have a new birth of freedom, and we are going to keep democratic government. We will make sure to keep alive the concept that government is created by the citizens for their own benefit.*

Compared to:

> *This nation, under God, shall have a new birth of freedom—and that government (1) of the people, (2) by the people, (3) for the people, shall not perish from the earth. (I added the numbers; but you probably figured that out.)*

STEP 8: USE HUMOR WHEN APPROPRIATE

Nothing falls as flat as inappropriate humor, but when used properly a little levity not only gets your point across but actually gives you a little leeway in forcefully expressing a point.

First, let's deal with the issue of appropriateness. In the workplace, you have to navigate some treacherous waters when using humor, because some people are basically humorless and won't get or appreciate *anything*. Second, modern society has evolved a permanent contingency of the perpetually indignant.

Having said that, there is a type of humor that almost always works: relevant and self-deprecating. Let me use an example of spoken, not written, humor; the approach could just as easily be used in written communication.

One of my professors when I was an undergraduate taught a large lecture class and began the first class of the semester by taking attendance and reading the names from a roster. Some of the names were challenging, and of course many names had pronunciations that were hard to guess. He invariably butchered a couple of names and asked for the correct pronunciation.

After the third act of butchery he recalled how he began his career as a television announcer, and learned that a cardinal rule of saying an unfamiliar name on the air is to first make every effort to learn the correct pronunciation, but if you can't, *never hesitate* before you pronounce it. If you hesitate, you'll sound wrong, even if you are right.

He then recalled the time when, as a TV reporter, he had to fill in at the last minute when the sports announcer fell ill. He was required to read, with no time to check out the pronunciations, a list of current boxing champions. He did all right with names like Larry Holmes and Marvin Hagler, but when he got to lightweights, mostly international boxers with names like Sot Chitalada and Jorge Ahumada, he just barreled through and brazenly bluffed. He even added the lilt of a foreign inflection as he grew bolder.

He was pulling it off, but the camera crew dissolved into a fit of laughter when he announced a bantamweight champion as a "tough little scrapper" he phoneticized as TEET-lay Vah-CAHT-ed. He of course added a confident bit of Spanish inflection to the name, which of course was actually "Title Vacated." (Here he wrote "Title Vacated" on the chalkboard.)

He used the joke at the beginning of every semester, and sometimes in public appearances where he had to meet and address people with unfamiliar names. The joke invariably worked, or at least never failed. Even if it fizzled or most people don't get it, the joke is *a relevant part of the presentation* and there is a reason for it to be there—unlike the awkward and all-too-common scenario where a novice speaker suddenly inserts an irrelevant story about a horse walking into a bar.[10]

The humor is at the expense of the person telling the joke, so there's no reason for anyone to become indignant.

As to my contention that humor can actually give you some leeway in making your strong feelings heard: Humor allows you to make a point but be able to back away from it, saying, in effect, "I'm only kidding." Satirists have known about this escape clause for centuries. For example, Jonathan Swift wrote a light-hearted fable called *Gulliver's Travels* that was really a series of jabs at British bureaucrats. A straightforward critique might have landed him in jail, but humor provided him with leeway and an out: "I was only kidding."

Look at what comedians routinely joke about and imagine what kind of response they would get if they covered the same issue in a heavy-handed, non-humor polemic. Torches and pitchforks would surely be involved.

With deft humor you can also defuse a situation; the joke, in effect, compels people to take themselves a little less seriously.

Adlai Stevenson was noted for his use of humor. He was an eloquent communicator—better at writing than at winning presidential elections, actually—and knew how to use humor, making him a difficult man not to like.

When he was governor of Illinois, Stevenson was confronted with the necessity of vetoing a loopy bill that would have allowed trapping cats who wandered off owners' property in order to save birds who would otherwise have been engaged in their civic duty of killing insects. Stepping into the eternal bird-cat controversy would ordinarily have compelled a lesser politician to greatly inflame one or the other overheated constituency. But Stevenson not only constructed a classic argument (state your case, give examples, refute your opponent's argument, state your conclusion, techniques explained in Chapter 7) but defused the dispute via some gentle and humorous needling. His humor used exaggerated formality—such as noting that cats have little "regard for property lines"—to make his fundamental point about the futility of the measure. He also made a compelling argument along the way. It's a long piece, but worth reprinting and reading in its entirety:

> *To the Honorable, the Members of the Senate of the Sixth-sixth General Assembly:*
>
> *I herewith return, without my approval, Senate Bill No. 93, entitled, "An Act to Provide Protection to Insectivorous Birds by Restraining Cats." This is the so-called "Cat Bill." I veto and withhold my approval from this Bill for the following reasons:*
>
> *It would impose fines on owners or keepers who permitted their cats to run at large off their premises. It would permit any person to capture or call upon the police to pick up and imprison cats at large. It would permit the use of traps. The bill would have statewide application—on farms, in villages, and in metropolitan centers.*
>
> *This legislation has been introduced in the past several sessions of the Legislature, and it has, over the years, been the source of much comment—not all of which has been in a serious vein. It may be that the General Assembly has now seen fit to refer it to one who can view it with a fresh outlook. Whatever the reasons for passage at this session, I cannot believe there is a widespread public demand for this law or that it could, as a practical matter, be enforced.*
>
> *Furthermore, I cannot agree that it should be the declared public policy of Illinois that a cat visiting a neighbor's yard or crossing the highway is a public nuisance. It is in the nature of cats to do a certain amount of unescorted roaming. Many live with their owners in apartments or other restricted premises, and I doubt if we want to make their every brief foray an opportunity for a small game hunt by zealous citizens—with traps or otherwise. I am afraid this Bill could only create discord, recrimination and enmity. Also consider the owner's dilemma: To escort a cat abroad on a leash is against the nature of the cat, and to permit it to venture forth for exercise unattended into a night of new dangers is against the nature of the owner. Moreover, cats perform useful service, particularly in rural areas, in combating rodents—work they necessarily perform alone and without regard for property lines.*
>
> *We are all interested in protecting certain varieties of birds. That cats destroy some birds, I well know, but I believe this legislation would further*

but little the worthy cause to with its proponents give such unselfish effort. The problem of cat versus bird is as old as time. If we attempt to resolve it by legislation who knows but what we may be called upon to take sides as well in the age old problems of dog versus cat, bird versus bird, or even bird versus worm. In my opinion, the State of Illinois and its local governing bodies already have enough to do without trying to control feline delinquency.

For these reasons, and not because I love birds the less or cats the more, I veto and withhold my approval from Senate Bill No. 93.[11]

You can't help but laugh, and you also can't help but agree.

STEP 9: INCLUDE LINGO AND INSIDE INFORMATION THAT INTRIGUE THE READER AND OFFER A GLIMPSE INTO OTHER PEOPLE'S THOUGHTS AND ACTIONS

People's choice of words often give us a profound insight into the way they think about their work, themselves, and others.

When you are writing about various lifestyles or professions, take note of the lexicon that is peculiar to them. It's interesting, is sometimes funny, and almost always offers an insight not normally glimpsed by the casual observer.

For example, the term "helicopter parent" is well known now, but when it was first introduced the sardonic nature of the term not only gave us a view of a particular type of person who persistently bugs teachers but also gave us an insight into teachers' attitudes toward a relentlessly hovering guardian.

You can enliven your writing by noting that, for example, the air-crash investigators nickname the process of their probe as "kicking tin," and that they look for clues called "Easter Eggs." Homicide detectives call a body in the water a "floater."

Sometimes the lingo (lingo means jargon or dialect particular to a group of people, often a group in a profession) is so fascinating that it can open the door to an entire story. Did you know, for example, that fast-food hamburger chains have a term for their most profitable customers? As Jennifer Ordonez reported in the *Wall Street Journal*:

In the vernacular of the fast-food industry, Mr. Sheridan is a heavy user. The heavy user accounts for only one of five fast-food patrons—but about 60% of all visits to fast-food restaurants. By this definition, the heavy user accounted for roughly $66 billion of the $110 billion the National Restaurant Association says was spent on fast food last year in the U.S.[12]

As the story points out, while the industry routinely calls them "heavy users," they don't do so to their faces.

STEP 10: STREAMLINE YOUR STYLE WITH STRONG SENTENCE STRUCTURE

I am ending this section on style on the topic of sentence structure for two reasons: First, I got a chance to come up with another clever accessible alliteration for the heading—four words this time. But more importantly, strong and inventive sentence structure not only makes your message clear and accessible but also is a style element within itself, lending drama and weight to your writing.

Sentence structure also becomes part of your individual writing voice. Hemingway, for example, is known for his short, declarative sentences. Tom Wolfe evidences a captivating, almost musical writing style with longer, meandering sentences that introduce sudden elements of surprise.

You can and should adapt the successful sentence structures of writers you admire to your own work, a concept scientifically defined as "stealing" that will be addressed in Chapter 10, Step 1. At this point, let me offer three fundamental suggestions about using sentence structure to make your writing come alive with vivid style.

One: Vary your sentence construction patterns. Short subject-verb-object sentences are fine. Feel free to use them. They are accurate and easy to understand. But after a while they get boring. They become hypnotic. Are you still with me? I doubt it. I've made. My point.

Two: Use as little of the passive voice as possible. The active voice is preferable because it adds forward motion and animation to writing. Active voice means when the subject of the sentence performs the action.

Members of the committee made mistakes.

The definition of passive voice can get complex, but in most cases it means when the object of the sentence is acted on by the subject, often via the use of the word "by":

Mistakes were made by members of the committee.

The passive voice is a favorite of writers who want to write in a vague, mushy style. Because a passive-voice sentence does not require identification of the actor, you can form a complete sentence without ever saying *who made* the mistake—hence, the classic statement, the last resort of elected officials everywhere:

Mistakes were made.

Three: Let your short sentences carry the weight. This is a very powerful stylistic device and easy to use because it's difficult to overdo. Also, employing this strategy doesn't call attention to itself.

Pick the thought you want to stress, the impression you want to leave behind, or the punch you want to land after setting your opponent up with a series of jabs. Put it in a short sentence.

Why? Short sentences *carry the impact*. Notice how jokes never have long punch-lines. Re-read Murrow's wartime reporting example in Step 3 and observe how "These things must be experienced to be understood" perfectly summed up flavor of the piece and how any attempt at making the sentence longer would have ruined it. And remember that General MacArthur is not revered for saying,

> *The President of the United States ordered me to break through the Japanese lines and proceed from Corregidor to Australia for the purpose, as I understand it, of organizing the American offensive against Japan, a primary objective of which is the relief of the Philippines.*

The pithy part of his statement came at the end, the important, punchy, and short part, the part we all remember:

> *I came through and I shall return.*

Chapter 5

Don't Turn Off the Reader by Making Dumb Mistake's with You're Grammar and Usage

A grammatical error robs your writing of credibility. No matter how inventive your writing is, or how profound your thought, an apostrophe error or some other type of obvious and easily avoidable mistake can make you appear uneducated. Your boss might not trust you on assignments that require verbal interaction, or an editor may be skeptical of your entire body of work because—in his or her view—someone who can't get basic grammar straight can't be trusted to report on potentially controversial issues.

I purposely located this chapter at the midpoint of the book because I wanted you to see how easily you could move your writing to a new level before introducing what may seem to some like dull material. I happen to like grammar but most normal and well-adjusted people find it tedious.

Having said that, I can provide you with ten basic steps that can help you fend off the majority of common grammar errors.

This section is not, by any means, a complete course in grammar nor is it intended to serve as one. It represents what I believe, based on my semi-scientific surveys of writing errors (which have a margin of error of plus or minus one hundred percent), to be the most common errors committed by people who otherwise write competently.

In the Suggested Readings at the end of this book I recommend a couple of excellent resources for those who want to learn more about grammar.

STEP 1: USE APOSTROPHES TO INDICATE POSSESSION—BUT KNOW THE HANDFUL OF EXCEPTIONS

No element of written English is as persistent a bugaboo as the apostrophe. If you take nothing else away from this section, or the entire book, for that matter, learn the basic rules of apostrophe use. I've seen manuscripts rejected and resumes tossed because of apostrophe errors. Don't let this happen to you.

All apostrophes do is to indicate *possession* and *missing letters*. We'll cover missing letters in the next entry.

Here is the low-down on possession: If the car belongs to Bob, it is *Bob's car*. If you are discussing the value possessed by a house, it is the *house's value*. When someone or something owns or possesses something else, you indicate possession by putting an apostrophe and an s after the name of the person who does the owning or the thing that does the possessing.

Another way to think of this is to see if the sentence equates to an "of" or "of the" statement. Is it the "value *of the* house?" Then it's a possessive. Is it the car of my son? It's a possessive—"my son's car."

If the person or thing that owns or possesses is plural, you put the apostrophe at the end of the word, after the final s. In other words, just make the plural with an s as you normally would and then add the apostrophe.

For example, if you are writing about the value of several houses, you would write:

The houses' value (the value of the houses)

If you are indicating possession by someone whose name ends in s, you have a choice:

James's car
James' car

Certain types of publications and some companies have style guide-books that specify one form or another when pluralizing proper names that end in s. You're safe with either, but in general, you're probably better off using *James's car* for writing in more formal venues, where the usage tends to be preferred.

Equally important is how **not** to use an apostrophe.

Do not use an apostrophe to indicate a plural.

> *NO: I own two car's.*

This is sometimes sneeringly referred to as a "greengrocer's plural" because you sometimes see it on signs in grocery stores—"apple's—two for a dollar!"

Do not use an apostrophe to indicate the possessive form of *it*. Here is how you form the possessive form of *it*.

> *Its = possession: its impact means* the impact of it.
> *It's = a contraction for* it is; the apostrophe replaces missing letters.

Never write *its'*. That word doesn't exist.

Do not use an apostrophe for the possessive form of who. Here are the correct usages:

> Whose = Possession: *Whose car is in the lot?*
> Who's = Who is. *Who's going to dinner?*

Do not use an apostrophe to make the possessive of *you* or any possessive pronoun. As mentioned earlier, *its* (when used as a possessive pronoun) has no apostrophe. *Yours* has no apostrophe. Neither does *his, hers,* or *mine.*

Also, **do not make a plural** to indicate possession. In other words, don't forget the apostrophe to show possession.

> *NO: This law violates a persons rights.*
> *NO: The addition adds to the houses value.*

There are two exceptions to these rules, both infrequent. If you are making a plural of a single letter, such as *dotting your I's,* some style books (sets of rules for journalists, grammarians, researchers, and others) say it's appropriate to use an apostrophe to indicate a plural. You can also use an apostrophe to pluralize a single number, such as, "the researchers threw out all the number 7's from the questionnaire." Sometimes various sources allow usage of apostrophes to pluralize abbreviations (*there is a shortage of MD's in the county*) or dates (the 1800's) but you're better off not doing this.

When a possessive becomes part of a commonly used name place or item made up of two words, such as *mens room, womens wear,* some sources say it's acceptable to omit the apostrophe. Again, I advise against this practice. Not every reader will be aware of the exceptions; play it safe.

STEP 2: USE APOSTROPHES TO INDICATE MISSING LETTERS

Step 1 demonstrated two common examples of apostrophes that indicate missing letters: it's and who's.

It's, of course, is a contraction for *it is,* and *who's* is a contraction for *who is.*

Some uses of apostrophes in contractions are less obvious as devices to indicate missing letters. O'clock, for example, is a contraction for "of the clock."

Generally, the use of apostrophes in contractions is not a difficulty for most writers. What is a problem is mixing up the contraction and possessive forms of the words discussed in the preceding entry:

It's/its
Who's/whose

In sum: there's no alternative but to memorize the rules of using apostrophes and the exceptions to the rules. That's the bad news. The good news is that the rules are pretty straightforward and the exceptions are few.

STEP 3: MAKE YOUR SUBJECTS AND VERBS AGREE IN NUMBER

Subject-verb agreement is fairly easy to figure out with short and simple sentences, but it becomes tricky when the sentence contains several clauses.

Subject-verb agreement means that if you have a singular subject you use a singular verb, or if you have a plural subject you use a plural verb or verb phrase.

Singular: The ship is headed into a storm.
Plural: The ships are headed into a storm.

But it becomes a puzzle when you add in a phrase between the subject and the verb. What do you put in the blank?

The ship, carrying hundreds of people, _____ headed into a storm.

You would use the word "is." Why? Because "ship" is the subject, and will always be the subject regardless of how many phrases are stuck between "ship" and the verb.

Yes, it gets tricky. But remember, no matter how tempting, *don't seize on the last noun before the verb and assume it's the subject. Just because the noun is near the verb doesn't mean it is the subject.*

Here's a sentence that tempts you to pick the wrong subject.

The president, along with a dozen members of his staff, _____ visiting the Kremlin.

Use "is." The president is the subject.

How do you find the subject? Look for the person or thing that is doing something. If it's still not clear, cross out the phrases that, used by themselves, will not make a complete sentence.

Here's what I mean:

The ship, carrying hundreds of people, is headed into the storm.

If you cross out "the ship," you don't have a real sentence:

Carrying hundreds of people, is headed into the storm.

Cross out "carrying hundreds of people," and you do have a complete sentence:

The ship is headed into the storm.

Another example:

The president, along with his staff, is visiting the Kremlin.

Cross out "the president" and you don't have a sentence:

Along with his staff, is visiting the Kremlin.

Cross out "along with his staff," and you have a real sentence, indicating that "The president" is the subject.

The president is visiting the Kremlin.

Here are some additional guidelines that will help with the most common subject-verb agreement issues.

When you use "or" in the subject, the verb or verb phrase will be singular.

Bob or Bill is likely to be elected.

Of course, if the subject is plural (called a "compound subject"), the verb is plural. In the preceding sentence, it was a choice of Bob (singular) or Bill (singular). But in the following sentence, the subject is both of them, Bob and Bill, a couple.

Bob and Bill are on the ticket together.

"None" means "not one" and takes a singular.

None of the candidates is electable.

Collective nouns (nouns that refer to a group) take a singular verb:

The group of demonstrators is headed toward the capital.

There are other variations of subject-verb agreement puzzles, but what I've presented here are in my judgment the most commonly confused subject-verb agreement scenarios.

STEP 4: AVOID "OUR SALESPEOPLE DO NOT HAVE QUOTAS BECAUSE THEY ARE UNPRODUCTIVE" AND OTHER HAZARDS OF VAGUELY REFERENCED PRONOUNS

Vague pronoun references lead to uncertainty and sometimes mistaken assumptions:

Bob fired Darrell because he is prejudiced.

You can read that sentence either way—either Bob is prejudiced or Darrell is. We don't know whom the "he" refers to. You can fix the confusion by eliminating the pronoun and using the name.

Bob fired Darrell because Darrell is prejudiced.

You could fix the example used as the title of this section (as God is my witness, somebody I know actually wrote that) by taking out the "they" and inserting the noun that is unproductive. The writer, of course, meant that "quotas" are unproductive.

Vague pronouns are a particular problem in business writing because they can lead to misunderstandings.

It will be an easy choice between product A and product B because it is simply inferior.

Remember again, readers can only read what you write. They cannot read your mind. Be sure that every pronoun is referenced clearly. If there is any doubt, replace it with a noun. Yes, a string of nouns or names may make the sentence seem clunky and repetitive, but that's a price you may have to pay to ensure clarity.

A related problem centers on agreement in number when using pronouns that are gender-specific. Modern usage trends generally don't condone using exclusively male modifiers in situations that refer to both genders.

When someone writes a paper he should research first.

There are a few fixes for this particular agreement in number problem, none of them perfect. The first is to use "he or she" relentlessly, which becomes instantly tedious. The second is to alternate "he" and "she" throughout the work. That can work, but you need a long enough passage to demonstrate that you are alternating. The third alternative is to use so-called inclusive language, which means intentionally mixing the forms of the nouns and pronouns.

When someone writes a paper they should research first.

Conventions in language are agreed upon—they don't exist in nature—but the jury is still out on this strategy. I would avoid it. It looks wrong because technically it is.

The fourth and, I believe, preferable way is to simply recast the entire sentence.

When people write a paper they should research first.

There are situations where this strategy can produce a stretched or stilted result, but you can generally work around the problem with an imaginative recasting of the wording.

Not all languages have gender-specific singular pronouns. The use of "he" to indicate a situation that involves both sexes derives from Anglo-Saxon usage several centuries ago. Therefore, direct your complaints to the Angles and Saxons who invented this issue.

STEP 5: USE COMMAS, PROPERLY WHEN SETTING OFF CLAUSES, INTRODUCTORY ELEMENTS, AND LISTS—NOT FOR RANDOM DECORATION AS AFTER THE SECOND WORD OF THIS SENTENCE

Commas are essential for understanding sentences because they cue us to where phrases begin and end and also separate items in groupings.

Commas in the wrong place are a distraction, and missing commas can muddy the meaning of what you write.

Here are the bare bones of how to use commas properly.

One important use of a comma is to set apart phrases that add information to the sentence but are not essential to the sentence structure itself.

The building, which features classic art-deco design, is scheduled to be demolished.

"Which features classic art-deco design" is a clause, a part of the sentence that is added in and is not entirely essential to the sentence. (Note that I am using the word "clause" loosely here; it has specific and tightly drawn meaning in formal grammar, but for our purposes the informal reference will do.) The commas set the clause apart from the sentence and enhance clarity.

The rule is: Put commas on both sides of a clause.

Don't do this: *The building which features classic art-deco design, is scheduled to be demolished.*

And don't do this: *The building, which features classic art-deco design is scheduled to be demolished.*

Another use of a comma is to put a break in a long compound sentence—meaning a sentence where there are separate thoughts expressed and one of the thoughts is in a phrase that is not a complete sentence.

Although both division heads endorsed the idea, the merger of the departments was scuttled when it was learned that there were serious tax consequences.

You have some leeway on the use of a comma to break up a compound sentence. You don't necessarily need a comma in shorter compound sentences.

Although it was initially approved the idea was eventually scuttled.

But whatever you do, don't throw in a comma when it serves no purpose in setting off a clause.

Don't do this: *Both division heads, endorsed the idea even though it would have created serious tax consequences.*

And never use a comma to join two complete sentences. That's called a run-on sentence or a comma splice, and will be explained in the next entry.

A comma is also used to set off a quote:

"We have to deal with this immediately," said Dr. Everett, "or there's no guarantee of a positive result."

Always put commas within quotation marks, as in the preceding example.

And a comma is employed to separate things in a list.

I have nothing to offer but blood, toil, tears and sweat.

The question of whether there should be a comma after the last item in the list is, believe it or not, a vigorously debated issue among grammarians, editors, and other people who have a lot of time on their hands.

A comma used at the end of a series, before the "and," is called a *serial comma*, or sometimes an *Oxford comma*.

Some people use a serial comma and others don't. It often depends on what "style" you are following, meaning the guidebook used by your profession or publisher. In news, journalists generally follow the lead of the Associated Press stylebook and the *New York Times* stylebook and omit the serial comma on the basis that it is unnecessary and clutters up the wording.

Without serial comma: *I have nothing to offer but blood, toil, tears and sweat.*

Several academic style guides, such as the *Chicago Manual of Style* and, not surprisingly, the *Oxford Style Manual*, instruct the writer to use the serial comma.

With serial comma: *I have nothing to offer but blood, toil, tears, and sweat.*

Personally, I favor the serial comma because omitting the final comma can, in rare circumstances, create confusion. Here's a joke grammarians swap among themselves when they really want to cut loose:

With serial comma: *We invited the strippers, JFK, and Stalin.*

But without the serial comma it appears that JFK and Stalin will finish the night naked:

Without serial comma: *We invited the strippers, JFK and Stalin.*

And sometimes the lack of a serial comma can produce some real-life puzzlers, such as a December 10, 2013, dispatch from the British news agency Sky News, which told readers that the top stories of the day were:

> "*World leaders at Mandela tribute, Obama-Castro handshake and same-sex marriage date set . . .*"

Interesting.

STEP 6: DO NOT COMPOSE RUN-ON SENTENCES, THEY ARE VERY AMATEURISH

A sentence cannot have two independent clauses—that is, two complete sentences joined by a comma. For example,

I went to the store, I bought bread.

. . . is a run-on because both sides of the comma can stand as complete sentences. This is sometimes called a "comma splice." You can fix it by making one side a dependent clause (an incomplete sentence):

When I went to the store, I bought bread.
I went to the store, and I decided to buy bread.

You can also easily fix a run-on by chopping it into two separate sentences.

Do not compose run-on sentences. They are very amateurish.

STEP 7: KNOW THE PROPER USAGE OF QUOTATION MARKS, SEMICOLONS, AND EXCLAMATION POINTS (AVOID THEM!)

Misused and misbegotten quotation marks, semicolons, and exclamation points are common distractions in writing and detract from the impact and respectability of your prose.

Here are guidelines for these three troublesome areas:

The primary appropriate use of quotation marks is to indicate that you are reprinting exact wording:

"The first order of business is to eliminate waste," Johnson said.

Quotation marks are also properly used to indicate slang, jargon, or unusual figures of speech.

The passenger was booked under a system called flight manifest, which the agents referred to as "flimming."

Quotation marks must "never" be used for emphasis, as humorist Dave Barry once warned in helpful column:

Another important grammar concept to bear in mind when creating hand-lettered small-business signs is that you should put quotation marks around random words for decoration, as in "TRY" OUR HOT DOG'S, or even TRY "OUR" HOT DOG'S.[1]

Semicolons are typically used to join two closely related sentences. In this sense, they are like commas on steroids because they can properly be used to mate two independent clauses.

The outcome was monumentally disappointing; the experimental group showed no improvement.

Sometimes semicolons are used to separate lists that already have commas:

The worst roads we encountered were in Rochester, Syracuse, and Buffalo during the winter; Miami, Tampa, and Orlando during the tourist season; and anywhere in West Texas when we needed a gas station.

Never use a semicolon to set off a list:

Wrong: Churchill promised the British only four things; blood, toil, tears, and sweat.

Use a colon (:) instead.

When in doubt, simply don't use a semi-colon. You are usually better off breaking up sentences so you don't need semicolons in the first place.

The outcome was monumentally disappointing. The experimental group showed no improvement.

Misuse of exclamation points is a hallmark of an amateurish writer. Having said that, they do have a place, often when used to show the intensity of the writer's emphasis, especially when used in a rhythmic way syncopating a discrete thought.

If you're really stuck, create a blank folder for the project. Anything! Having accomplished at least something today, you're facing a much less onerous task tomorrow because you'll be continuing the work, and not starting it.

But don't use them routinely! And for the love of all that is holy, never use more than one!!

When in doubt, leave the exclamation point out.

STEP 8: LEARN THE RULES FOR CHOOSING "WHICH VS. THAT," "WHO VS. WHOM," AND "LAY VS. LIE"

The rules of English grammar can be frustrating because some words can be correct when used in one context or position in a sentence, but incorrect when moved to in a slightly different position or given a different usage.

That and **which** are often confused. "Which" is used for a non-restrictive clause, meaning a part of a sentence that can be left out without "restricting," or changing the meaning of a sentence. Non-restrictive clauses are set off by commas.

The building, which features classic art-deco design, is scheduled to be demolished.

You can take the non-restrictive clause out and it still makes sense, although there is less information in the sentence.

The building is scheduled to be demolished.

"That" is used for a restrictive clause, meaning that the clause limits or "restricts" the meaning of the thing it refers to.

The building that is located on the corner of Jefferson and Main is scheduled to be demolished.

The location "restricts" the meaning to one building, and therefore takes the word "that" and does not use commas to set off the clause. Thousands of buildings have art-deco designs, so the clause is descriptive but not restrictive—it does not limit the meaning to one building—and takes the word "which."

The pronoun "who" is used when it is the subject of sentence. "Whom" is used when referring to the object of a sentence, usually pointed to with a preposition.

Subject: *Who went to the meeting?*
Object: *To whom am I speaking?*
Object: *Whom is Bob hiring? ("Whom" is the object, which becomes apparent when you recast the sentence to say, "Bob is hiring whom?")*

I will now earn the wrath of English teachers everywhere by saying that by and large not many people pay attention to the "who and whom" convention any more. My advice: If you err (and you probably will) err on the side of using "who." "Whom" can seem stuffy when used correctly, and laughably pretentious when used incorrectly.

Don't worry excessively. Confusing "who" and "whom," or, "that and which," in the grand scheme of things, is a minor violation.

But mixing up "lay" and "lie" is a misdemeanor. (For reference, using an apostrophe to make a plural is a felony.) Here is the proper meaning:

> *Lay means to put in place or put down.*
> *Lie means to recline.*

Here is "lay" in its common usages:

> *I will lay the bricks on the top row.*
> *I laid the bricks yesterday.*
> *I am laying a top layer of bricks on the patio.*

Here is "lie" in its common usages:

I will lie down in bed for half an hour.
I lay down this morning and overslept.
The bodies of the victims had lain in the shallow grave for years.

If nothing else, remember:

Do not write, "I was laying on the couch." When used to mean recline, the only use of lay is the past tense: "I lay down on the couch this morning."

STEP 9: AVOID THE "I SAW A MOOSE ON VACATION IN MAINE" CONUNDRUM AND OTHER HAZARDS OF A DANGLING MODIFIER (AND IF YOU CAN'T AVOID A DANGLING MODIFIER, FOLLOW JOHNNY CARSON'S ADVICE AND WEAR A LONG COAT)

A modifier is a word or phrase that describes or clarifies something. A dangling modifier comes about when it's not clear what word in the sentence is being described or clarified. Sometimes the thing being described is missing altogether:

Having received your request, the tiger will be housed farther from the barricade.

The writer meant something like, "The zoo administrator received your request, and has decided that a safety hazard does exist and the tiger will be housed farther from the barricade." The missing part was the fact that the zoo administrator was the one who received the letter.

Sometimes all the elements are there, but the sentence is unclear as to which element is being modified, as in Groucho Marx's famous example:

One morning I shot an elephant in my pajamas. How he got into my pajamas I'll never know.

Journalist and grammarian Constance Hale, who writes about language for the *New York Times*, collected a trove of dangling modifiers, including:

The company's refrigerator held microwavable lunches for 18 employees frozen in the top compartment.

Lost: Antique walking stick by an old man with a carved ivory head.

This is a Hybrid Multi-channel SACD, which plays on any CD player. However, when played on an SACD player, the listener will hear the exceptional audio resolution that only a DSD recording can provide.[2]

To avoid such howlers, be sure to put modifiers as close to the word being modified as possible. Or just make the overly complex sentence into two clear sentences.

Seared over an open flame, the chef prepared the juiciest steak I'd ever tasted.

The chef seared the steak over an open flame. It was the juiciest steak I'd ever tasted.

Modifier errors are particularly dangerous because they produce results that are not only ungrammatical but prompt people to laugh at you and sometimes post your e-mail on Facebook for everyone to laugh at. So fix this problem now; it is simply unacceptable to let modifiers dangle in polite society.

STEP 10: KEEP SENTENCE ELEMENTS PARALLEL, MAKE THE WORDING SIMILAR, AND LOOK DO YOU SEE HOW STUPID IT SOUNDS WHEN YOU DON'T?

This is a common problem but an easy fix.

When sentence elements go out of whack, you get a schizophrenic result:

Designers and programmers are able to offer online testing, metrics that track user participation, along with sophisticated video.

The reader isn't sure if the sentence means that the online testing includes metrics that track participation, or if the "along" means with the first two elements listed.

That's why it's important to re-read and edit anything before you publish or send it. It's easy to muddle sentence construction when you are thinking on the fly, as I did when I wrote that sentence in a recent e-mail about a training video project with which I'm involved.

I cleaned it up by making all the sentence elements parallel—meaning that each has the same internal construction:

Designers and programmers are able to offer online testing, implement metrics that track user participation, and produce sophisticated video.

What I mean by "internal construction" is that each of the three examples was stated with a verb—"offer," "implement," and "produce."

Chapter 6

Use Concrete Examples, Explanations, and Evidence to Reinforce Your Point (Speaking of Concrete, the Hoover Dam Used Enough Concrete to Build a Road from New York to California)

Examples are the hard currency of entertaining, evocative, and persuasive writing. Without real-life nuggets, prose becomes overly abstract and lifeless. This section shows how to craft compelling examples and use them to maximum benefit.

An advanced form of example use is the anecdote, a story that not only serves as an example but tells a story related to the overall point you are trying to make. Anecdotes will be discussed in detail in Chapter 8, Step 2.

STEP 1: USE EXAMPLES THAT RELATE TO EVERYDAY LIFE

The Hoover Dam was constructed with 6.6 million tons of concrete. I realize that's a lot but I don't really know what a million tons of concrete looks like. So that's essentially a yawner in my book.

But 6.6 million tons of concrete is enough to build a road from New York to California. I know what a road looks like, and I have a pretty good idea that New York to California is a really long way.

In a similar vein, I could bombard you with numbers indicating the amount of steel used in constructing the Empire State Building, or I could provide an example that has more meaning: When it was being built, so much steel was needed that 500 trucks a day unloaded steel at the construction site—roughly one truck a minute. The schedule was so tight that if a truck missed its spot in line, the driver would have to wait about two days to complete the delivery.

Whenever possible—and it usually is—use the strategy illustrated earlier. Put your examples in terms that compare the scenario to something with which your reader is already familiar.

STEP 2: WHEN OFFERING EXPLANATIONS, DON'T DEFINE UNFAMILIAR CONCEPTS WITH UNFAMILIAR WORDS

Remember that if your reader needs an explanation of something, don't concoct an explanation that needs another explanation.

Here's an example of what I mean: "Lifting a dumbbell once is called a rep. When performing a rep, make sure to allow for more time on the negative than the positive."

A reader who doesn't know what a rep is probably won't know the difference between the positive part of the motion (lifting the weight up) and the negative (controlling its descent back to the original position).

Granted, there's no way to ascertain for sure what a group of readers knows and doesn't know, but if you are the expert you should have some idea of the knowledge level of the majority of readers. Assuming you can gauge that, the trick now is to *keep the level of sophistication of the words in your explanation consistent.*

Here's an example of finding the right level and staying consistent: If I were writing an article about knee pain for a medical trade journal (a magazine intended for members of a certain profession), I'd have no reluctance to use the words "anterior" and "posterior" to describe the front and back of the knee. But for a general-interest publication, I'd stick to "front" and "back," and if I had a quote from someone using those words, I would explain their meaning in the narrative. While I might not draw up an actual list, I would keep tabs on the overall level of language used in the articles. Here's what I would use in a trade journal vs. a newspaper article.

Trade Journal	Newspaper
Anterior	Front
Posterior	Back
Patella	Kneecap
Abrasion	Scrape
Contusion	Bruise
Repetitive stress injury	Injury from overuse
Hyperflexion	Flexing beyond the normal range

Now, here's the real point of all this: For illustration, mentally compose a couple of sentences that use words from the "newspaper" column but had one ringer from the "trade journal" column. Try the reverse exercise; while you won't anticipate trouble with reader comprehension, the effect is jarring.

When in doubt, use less jargon and more plain English and throw in a generous number of definitions. That was the approach I took in the section on grammar, and I don't think it seemed simplistic or dumbed down. The takeaway: Keep your explanations accessible because readers can usually tolerate something they consider obvious but will rebel at an explanation that leaves them perplexed.

STEP 3: PUT IN ENOUGH BACKGROUND SO THAT MOST READERS UNDERSTAND CONTEXT—BUT DON'T OVERLOAD

Sometimes an explanation won't tell the whole story until it's grounded in context.

The fact that a computer system at a government office crashed is important—but what's the context? Was it the fifth time this month? Were people who had business at the office turned away?

We have a tendency to bury explanatory material at the end of a piece or in one clump somewhere in the middle. That strategy can be tolerated, but it's clunky and overloads the reader with a textbook-style chunk of force-fed instruction all in one gulp. Instead, try adding background and context bit-by-bit.

Here is an excellent excerpt from an explanatory piece in which the *New York Times*' Dennis Overbye provides background and context through an easily grasped opening and dollops of information dropped into an engaging narrative:

Mario Livio tossed his car keys in the air.

They rose ever more slowly, paused, shining, at the top of their arc, and then in accordance with everything our Galilean ape brains have ever learned to expect, crashed back down into his hand.

That was the whole problem, explained Dr. Livio, a theorist at the Space Telescope Science Institute here on the Johns Hopkins campus.

A decade ago, astronomers discovered that what is true for your car keys is not true for the galaxies. Having been impelled apart by the force of the Big Bang, the galaxies, in defiance of cosmic gravity, are picking up speed on a dash toward eternity. If they were keys, they would be shooting for the ceiling.

"That is how shocking this was," Dr. Livio said.

It is still shocking. Although cosmologists have adopted a cute name, dark energy, for whatever is driving this apparently antigravitational behavior on the part of the universe, nobody claims to understand why it is happening, or its implications for the future of the universe and of the life within it, despite thousands of learned papers, scores of conferences and millions of dollars' worth of telescope time. It has led some cosmologists to the verge of abandoning their fondest dream: a theory that can account for the universe and everything about it in a single breath.[1]

STEP 4: UTILIZE EXAMPLES OF BEHAVIOR THAT SHOW THE SUBJECT'S PERSONALITY AND CHARACTER DEVELOPMENT

We often forget to use examples that illuminate the nature of the people who populate our writing. Using such illustrations is a simple, powerful, and immediate way to cement the connection between you and your reader.

I once worked for a publication edited by Dr. Rushworth M. Kidder, the former features editor of the *Christian Science Monitor* who went on to found the influential Institute for Global Ethics. Kidder had a rule that every profile piece he edited include a brief physical description of the room or environment in which the interview was conducted, a description of the person being interviewed, and some action on the part of the subject of the piece (not all at once, of course, but sprinkled throughout the profile).

That's a good rule, and I've occasionally imposed it on students and journalists whose work I edit.

The physical description of the locale makes the piece seem more real in the theater of the mind, and sometimes it adds some insight into the situation or the person who is the subject. For example, it's interesting to note that Michael Bloomberg, the former New York City mayor, worked in an open office at City Hall, a desk in the middle of a sea of other desks, a setup that resembled a stock trading floor more than a mayor's office. You can't read too much into it, but the environment he created does speak to his background and management style, and perhaps to the image he wants to project to constituents.

Describing the subject of the piece is a no-brainer, but I've seen some pretty brainless writing where there is not a word of description and the reader is left in a vacuum. One piece I edited actually featured a subject with an androgynous name—I think it was Jamie—with no hint as to whether the subject was male or female. Such detachment makes the piece seem distant and secondhand. A brief phrase—"a trim man in his fifties with short, grey hair, cut military-style"—provides the reader with a picture of who is talking and cuts through some of the fog and distance.

As to actions: Does the person you are writing about habitually stand when someone comes into a room? Speak with low intensity? Interrupt others constantly? Make sweeping gestures? Focus intently on one person while screening out hubbub in the immediate environment? Drum fingers? All are telling actions and gestures.

Here's an example of how actions can provide insight. It's from Kalyce Rogers, a young writer who publishes on the blogging platform Medium, which has evolved into a venue for some truly outstanding writing by emerging authors:

> *I know he's got at least some money, because he's buying Grey Goose. People with money don't buy cheap vodka, or cheap rum, or cheap whiskey. They invest in the good stuff, like Grey Goose. Three bottles of it.*
>
> *His suit radiates "expensive," the kind of expensive that involves several tailors and a high-end store in Manhattan. We aren't in Manhattan, though. We're in a fluorescent-lit Ralph's in a suburban city that sleeps from 10 PM to 6 AM. Men who belong in Manhattan look out of place here.*
>
> *"How are you doing tonight, sir?" The woman working the register asks pleasantly enough. My eyes are fixated on her hands, veins prominent through tired skin, as they scan bottle after bottle. His own fingers drum on the register wall impatiently. A gold band catches lights and gleams from his ring finger.*
>
> *"Fine. Now, if you wouldn't mind speeding up this damn process, I've got places to be." He snaps, taking a black leather wallet out of his jacket pocket, a shiny credit card protruding from the top. It looks like it's made of silver. He holds it gingerly between his index finger and middle finger, and now that his hands are busy, he begins tapping his foot on the linoleum. There is a faint, distinct rhythm, but I can't place where I've heard it before.*[2]

Example, example, example! The behavior, more than the description, gives the piece reality and vibrancy.

STEP 5: WHEN USING NUMBERS, ROUND THEM OFF WHEN APPROPRIATE

Numbers are among the most powerful examples at our disposal because they are "hard" and "don't lie." I put those descriptors in quotes as figures of speech out of sarcasm, of course, because numbers *do* lie, as I'll demonstrate in the following entries, but an honest number put in proper context can be a brawny component of your writing.

But the problem with numbers is that they tend to hypnotize. A cascade of numbers, especially long numbers and decimals, becomes a blur.

In general, you can increase readability by rounding off numbers when there is no particular need for precision. For example, a "two-and-a-half million dollar budget" gets the idea across as well as a "$2, 531,123.00 budget." Should you be writing a report on formulation of the budget in a company document you might want to use the precise number on the first reference, but round off if you refer to it again.

An especially useful tactic in simplifying numbers and making them more meaningful and memorable is to stress the relationships between and among numbers and *not the numbers themselves.* Instead of saying, "revenues rose from $1,534,000 to $3,110,000," write, "revenues almost doubled."

Percentages, even though they are usually expressed numerically, are easier for the reader to conceptualize than raw numbers. So do the math for your reader when using numerical examples:

A drop of ten percent . . .
An increase of nearly half . . .
One in three Americans will pay higher taxes . . .

STEP 6: WHEN USING NUMBERS, MAKE THEM INSTANTLY MEANINGFUL

James C. Humes wrote a wonderful book titled *Speak Like Churchill, Stand Like Lincoln: 21 Powerful Secrets of History's Greatest Speakers.* I heartily recommend it. (Almost all the advice given in the book applies to writing as well as speaking.)

Humes offered some effective techniques for making numbers meaningful. He notes, for example, that 623,000 soldiers were killed in the Civil War. Compelling and tragic, certainly, but what does that mean in context? He explains:

. . . what is more remembered is that the dead of the Civil War exceeded the lives lost in all the other wars the United States had fought: the Revolutionary War, the War of 1812, the Spanish-American War, World War I, World War II, the Korean War, the Vietnam War, and Desert Storm.[3]

Another way to make meaning out of numbers is by comparison. Humes remembers a speaker railing against excessive government regulation who arrayed numbers this way:

The Lord's Prayer has 66 words, the Ten Commandments 179 words, the Gettysburg Address 282 words. But do you know how many words are in the U.S. government's regulations on the sale of cabbage? 26,911 words![4]

Writer Paul Fussell quoted a journalist who created a comparison that put statistics about plane fatalities during air crashes in World War II into stark context:

The relative few who actually fought know that the war was not a matter of rational calculation. They know madness when they see it. They can draw the right conclusions from the fact that in order to invade the Continent the Allies killed 12,000 innocent French and Belgian civilians who happened to live in the wrong part of town—that is, too near the railway tracks, the bombers' target. The few who fought are able to respond appropriately—without surprise—to such a fact as this: in the Netherlands alone, more than 7,000 planes tore into the ground or the water, afflicted by bullets, flak, exhaustion of fuel or crew, "pilot error," discouragement, or suicidal intent. In a 1986 article in Smithsonian *magazine about archaeological excavation in Dutch fields and drained marshes, Les Daly emphasized the multitudinousness, the mad repetitiveness of these 7,000 crashes, reminding readers that "the total fighter and bomber combat force of the U.S. Air Force today amounts to about 3,400 airplanes. To put it another way, the crash of 7,000 aircraft would mean that every square mile of the entire state of New Jersey would have shaken to the impact of a downed plane."*[5]

STEP 7: DON'T CITE MISLEADING STATISTICS, AND DON'T BE FOOLED BY OTHER PEOPLE'S MISREPRESENTATIONS

A particular problem with numbers is that they seem scientific and accurate, but their spurious precision—the appearance of accuracy—can obscure a lot of tinkering.

I knew a radio station manager who asked a handful of people how long they listened to the station each day. Most shrugged and said something like "I don't know, two hours, I guess." Another said, "about three." Another guessed four. He added up the responses and crowed in his sales literature: "Our average listener tunes in for 3.6 hours per day!"

The precise number is a lot more persuasive than "I asked five people and they said somewhere between two and five hours."

I have an excruciatingly clever name for that type of statistical fallacy: precision garbage. You can toss a whopping pile of garbage into the calculation, but when it comes out, it is still garbage but has a specific-sounding number attached to it.

Statistical significance in sample sizes is far beyond the scope of this book, but for our purposes remember that you should always try to discern what went into the calculation of a precise-appearing statistic, such as the "survey" of radio listenership cited earlier.

What's left out of a statistic is often as important as what was put in. A few years ago the *Wall Street Journal* found that many universities were inflating their average SAT scores by leaving out groups of students who didn't score well, such as non-native speakers of English. Sometimes the universities just brazenly omitted their results; in other cases, administrators came up with some sort of subterfuge, such as admitting low-scoring students a few weeks earlier than the rest of the student population and using that as justification to take them off the books.

Also, watch out for statistics that mix apples and oranges. For example, you could make a claim like this:

> *The average person treated for a workplace-related injury by a chiropractor returned to work more quickly and spent less money on treatment than people who sought traditional medical care.*

Now, the "average" might be true, but it mixes two things that shouldn't be added together: people with minor injuries and people with major injuries. Someone who lost an arm to a power saw won't seek treatment from a chiropractor. He'll seek "traditional" medical care—a trauma surgeon, an emergency room, and maybe a helicopter ride—and spend hundreds of thousands of dollars. Averages can be true and lie at the same time.

Even the word "average" can be misleading. I once heard a school board candidate claim that something had to be done (insert sound effects of fist pounding on lectern) because "half the reading scores in the district were below average." *Of course* half were below average; that's usually what an average is—the point at which half are above and half are below.

Add to that the problem that the word "average" can—accurately—mean three different things:

The Mean   Add up everything and divide by the number of things you added.

The Median   The measurement in the middle of the other measurements, such as the sixth-highest measurement in a sample of 11.

The Mode   The most frequently occurring.

All measure a type of central tendency and all can legitimately be called "averages."

Each type of average has its uses and abuses. A mean, for example, can be misleading if the value of the things added up are widely divergent.

If there were ten houses sold in a town last month, and nine sold in the $200,000 range, but one was a mansion that sold for $4 million, the mean would inform you that the average house sold for about $580,000. That's technically accurate but deceptive.

Graphs can depict numbers in a deceptive way. Graphs, like numbers, give the impression of accuracy but can be profoundly misleading. I can take the same sales results and tinker with the left axis of the graph and produce a graphic that gives an entirely different perception of reality. Author Darrell Huff, who wrote *How to Lie with Statistics*, calls this a "Gee-Whiz graph."

If the left axis started at zero, the line would be practically flat. But by truncating the left axis, the line shoots skyward. You can see an example of the Gee-Whiz graph in the book proposal I include in Chapter 11. (It's included as an example of persuasive writing. The proposal, for *Lies We Live By*, dealt with various methods of statistical, numerical, and verbal misrepresentation.)

Challenge statistics. Try to determine if they have been concocted with precision garbage or veiled variables. Don't fall for a phony statistic, and don't pass one along yourself.

STEP 8: NEVER MAKE OR FALL FOR A SPURIOUS CAUSE-AND-EFFECT EXPLANATION AND KNOW HOW TO DEFLATE SUCH AN ARGUMENT IF IT IS USED AGAINST YOU

Be wary of any statistic or argument that implies a cause and effect. The existence of a statistical correlation (when one variable changes, the other variable changes) does not mean that one variable changing caused the effect.

Cause-and-effect fallacies are intoxicatingly alluring because they seem so obvious:

Married people live longer than unmarried people.

It stands to reason, then, that . . .

Getting married will cause you to live longer.

The linkage (correlation) is true, but does that establish *causation*? Maybe "loneliness kills," as more than one overheated magazine article has attested, citing the statistical correlations, but there are many other reasons why unmarried people die younger than those who are married:

- People with serious chronic childhood diseases die at a younger age and therefore don't get married as much as their healthy counterparts
- Many young men die in auto wrecks before they reach marriage age
- If you are using statistics that include times of war, unmarried men enlist and are drafted at a higher rate than married men, and, of course, die at a higher rate

When you are employing examples in your writing, or analyzing examples provided by others, be sure to give them the smell test if there is an implication of cause and effect. What you say may very well be true, but if your evidence doesn't back it up you are making a claim you can't prove.

For example, someone once wrote me this:

I support the construction of a light rail line through the region because in the line that was developed in a residential area in California property values went up all around the line. Who would oppose increasing their property values?

This statement makes two assumptions:

- Property values near light rail lines are linked, with property values going up when light rail is built.
- Therefore, building a light rail line *causes* an increase in property values.

Not so fast! The proposed line in my area was slated for a region with decreasing population; it was meant primarily as a connection between two commercial hubs.

The line in California, as is the case with most light rail lines, was built to accommodate large increases in population—in other words, they are built in areas where people are flocking and property values will go up regardless of whether there is a train.

So, it is almost certainly the case that property values typically go up in areas where light rail is built.

It *could* be the case, but *not necessarily the case based on the statistic,* that the property values in the example in question will go up.

If you have someone wielding a spurious cause-and-effect argument against you, there is a universal defense that never fails:

The rooster crows every morning.
And then, every morning, the sun comes up.
Does the rooster cause the sun to rise?

STEP 9: CHECK COMPARISONS TO MAKE SURE THEY ARE, IN FACT, COMPARABLE

While I am a fan of comparisons to put facts and figures into context, I am aware that comparisons can go haywire if not structured carefully, cohesively, and ethically.

Sometimes a faulty comparison is the result of simply not thinking things through. I remember reading an impassioned piece written in the aftermath of Hurricane Katrina that implied some obvious malfeasance among Southerners because up North where the author lived they had no trouble digging out. Having lived through both types of disasters, I can attest that the comparison is not valid. (Among other things, snow tends to stay outside when the doors and windows are shut.) As always, be careful of hasty assumptions when you write but be particularly wary about embedding those assumptions in comparisons.

Some comparisons are invalid because they draw a contrast with the nonexistent. I made a long-running joke out of bogus comparison when I described one of my books as "The Number One Bestseller by Carl Hausman!" There is an implicit comparison in that statement—that my book was number one compared to . . . to . . . to *what?*

That's called a *dangling comparative* and you have to guard against being fooled by the tactic. Dangling comparatives are ubiquitous. Just watch a few television commercials.

Gives you 30 percent more! (More than what?)
Twice as effective! (Twice what? Effective at doing what?)

My personal dangling comparative was used to promote my book *Lies We Live By*, an exposé about the ways phony statistics and misleading words are used in advertising, politics, and business. When questioned, I would point out that indeed *Lies* was the number-one bestseller by Carl Hausman: Among the eighteen other books Carl Hausman had written, it was the best seller. It's not my fault, I noted during the promotional tour for the book, if people fall prey to faulty comparisons and assumed it meant the number-one bestseller on, say, the *New York Times* list. If they are that gullible, they really need to buy the book.

STEP 10: BE JUDICIOUS WHEN USING POLL OR SURVEY DATA TO REINFORCE YOUR CONTENTIONS

We are awash in polls and surveys that purport to "prove" something.

When you are using poll data as examples, explanations, or evidence, tread carefully. You don't want to mislead readers or, from a pragmatic standpoint, be embarrassed if it turns out you have wielded specious evidence.

Most importantly, don't reify polling data as public opinion. ("Reify" is a great word, and while I mostly used it to show off, it also is the *perfect* word for the occasion, meaning to take an abstract concept and attempt to make it a material thing.) What I mean is that a poll is snapshot in time, and you have to be careful about trying to make a feature film out of it. A poll reflects a measure of what a certain group responded when asked a specific question. So be circumspect about saying, "most people believe X" when you should be saying, "according to a poll conducted on Nov. 13, 60 percent of respondents favored . . ."

A poll can be skewed in astonishing ways, by accident or by intention. An exercise I once assigned in public opinion classes I taught was fun and instructive: Half my class went out on the streets of New York City and asked, "Do you favor increasing benefits to veterans even though it will result in higher taxes." The other half asked, "Do you favor raising taxes in order to pay for increasing benefits to veterans?" When the word "veterans" came first, the poll results were overwhelmingly "yes." When the virtually identical question was asked with the word "taxes" first, the results were overwhelmingly "no."

You'd want to be careful, then, of using my poll to write that "people support increased veterans benefits." Or that they don't. Because they do *and* they don't, depending on how you ask them.

Remember, too, that polling often involves asking questions of people who don't know and don't care. You'd want to show considerable caution, for instance, in claiming that the political establishment thinks military aid to Fredonia is a good thing. A now-defunct but brilliant satire magazine named *Spy* once polled U.S. congressional representatives about support for Fredonia, pointing out, as part of the poll, that the president felt Fredonia was critical to U.S. interests. Many of the representatives polled heartily concurred—an interesting response considering that there is no country named Fredonia. It was the fictional setting of the Marx Brothers' movie *Duck Soup*.

Chapter 7

Use Simple and Proven Techniques of Persuasion If Your Aim Is to Motivate or Convince

Understanding the techniques of persuasion is clearly important if you are writing a sales brochure or a stock prospectus. But a great deal of writing, especially in the business world, is persuasive in nature even though you may not think of it as a sales pitch or a polemic. You may be subtly or overtly asking for resources, more respect for your message, or alignment with your general view.

Persuasive writing is an essential tool for getting what you want out of life. Unfortunately, many people simply don't understand what persuasion is. Seriously, they don't. Many believe that persuasion is winning an argument. That's wrong; you can trounce opposing arguments with facts and figures and clever comeuppances and still not persuade the people you have vanquished, or, for that matter, their followers. By "winning" an argument, you might even cement them more solidly in opposition to you.

The methods you use to persuade also depend on the situation. The wrong approach can be counterproductive.

With that in mind, here's what research and experience shows really works in the effort to win hearts and minds.

STEP 1: ASSESS YOUR AUDIENCE AND GAUGE YOUR PERSUASION ACCORDINGLY: REINFORCE THOSE WHO ARE LIKELY TO AGREE WITH YOU, PERSUASIVELY INFORM THOSE WHO ARE NEUTRAL, AND DEFLECT AND REDIRECT THOSE WHO DISAGREE

All persuasive writing doesn't have the same approach. Some is meant to edify opinion, and is aimed at people with whom you are essentially in agreement. For example, look at the columns of opinion writers for major publications and syndicates. Is there ever any shift in their opinion? Any surprise turn of ideology? Most likely not. They are assuredly preaching to the choir, but their adherents read them for the same reason the converted listen to sermons: to bolster and confirm their existing beliefs—perhaps to provide some additional evidence to firm up the opinions they already share.

Are you writing to the converted, hoping to galvanize the audience? It happens a lot, and it's an important function of persuasive communication. In the workplace, for example, you may be writing to stir up enthusiasm for a cause with which most people agree. If you're a journalist writing an opinion piece, you may be adding evidence and analysis useful for your readers and adherents. If you are a politician, you know that you are wasting your time trying to convert hard-core Democrats into hard-core Republicans or vice versa; that hardly ever happens. Your goal is to persuade people to actually go out in the rain to get into the polling place on Election Day.

Are your readers new to the debate? Readers are often neutral when an issue is new. This works to your advantage because ostensibly they will welcome the opportunity to be educated about your position. Combining persuasion with elucidation is powerful because readers consume (your) facts and your opinions in the same helping. There's an ethical line you must walk here, because it's dishonest to simply present facts that only back your case when "informing" readers. In fact, communication scholars who study propaganda call this technique "card stacking."

Having said that, you have a right to your opinion and a right to honestly advocate for your opinion. When writing for a readership you expect will agree with you or be open to persuasion to your point of view, the approach is to present your evidence, consider and dismiss conflicting claims (see Step 7), and tighten your arguments so that the reader is "funneled" into agreeing with you.

If your readership is likely to disagree with you, reinforcing existing beliefs is clearly a waste of time, and telling people they are wrong and then trying to change their view is not only pointless but counterproductive (as explained in Step 2). The most effective way to attempt to persuade a hostile readership is to use the same deflection and redirection technique a good salesperson uses: "I understand your objection, and one way we can overcome that . . ."

What you do in a hostile-reader situation is this: (1) *Acknowledge the objection,* (2) *don't belittle it,* and (3) *deflect the argument into another choice you offer the reader.* Here's an example: One of the most interesting pieces of persuasion I've encountered was a letter that came to me when I was on a local board considering land-use regulation. In a nutshell, the government wanted builders to install a sidewalk in front of houses planned for a new development. Builders don't like sidewalks. They are expensive and a nuisance to construct. But instead of writing, "sidewalks are expensive and hard to build and you are wrong to require me to do so," a builder used the three-prong technique, writing:

> *I do understand that there is a great need for sidewalks in high-traffic areas, with sidewalks being less of a necessity in more isolated developments. It is a dilemma builders confront often, and in many cases, such as the ones to be considered next week, I ask for the option of saving on sidewalk construction so that I may give the buyers, many of whom will be first-time homeowners, a little more house for their money.*

Do you see the cleverness embedded in this approach? The reader is not put on the defensive or told he or she is wrong. The reader's likely opinion is not denigrated. And then the reader is guided into an alternate choice that does not require the reader to admit being wrong in the first place, either to himself or others. The reader is also given a viable, defensible fallback position: "I decided to change my mind about the sidewalk issue so I could give first-time homebuyers a break."

Remember, when confronted with contrary positions, most people hunker down and defend their views, either explicitly—if directly confronted—or stealthily, by simply moving to the next article, channel, or conversation. So follow the additional strategies described in the next entry.

STEP 2: DON'T CONTRADICT THE READER'S OPINION AT THE BEGINNING

Some interesting studies bear out the danger of contradiction: Researchers tracked the eye patterns of subjects and found that when they were reading an article that initially supported their views, but then deliberately shifted viewpoints, the readers almost immediately lost interest and moved to another article.

When you are writing to persuade, you face the challenge of not driving away someone you eventually could convert to your opinion. But the most fundamental advice I can offer is what *not* to do: Do not begin with some variation of "you're wrong, and here's why." The sooner a reader is on the defensive, the harder the job of persuasion.

I know this was covered in the previous entry, but there is more to it. Remember when you write a piece with the goal of persuading, you do not share the same goal as a cable-TV news talking head: winning an argument with your reader is worthless. Sometimes, but not always, you can win an argument with a theoretical opponent and use that encounter to make your case.

Be careful about that tactic, though, because even unsophisticated readers can detect a "straw man" appeal. The straw man fallacy means that you have attacked an argument that your opponent really isn't making, or have mischaracterized your opponent's argument in a simplistic way, making it appear weak, and then refuted it.

Throughout any persuasive piece be cognizant of anything that may be backing readers into a corner. Don't attack directly. If you can't deflect and offer an alternative, attack the theoretical opponent but be sure not to knock down a straw man.

STEP 3: HAVE A CLEAR GOAL: ESTABLISH IN YOUR OWN MIND WHAT YOU WANT THE PERSUASIVE PIECE TO ACCOMPLISH

I'm aware that this admonition sounds like recycled self-help bromide—"You have to decide what you want and make a specific plan to get it." But bear with me, because this question is important and not at all obvious.

In persuasive communication you are trying to move an impactful share of readers from Point A in the opinion spectrum to Point B. You have to *identify Point A and Point B.* You're not going to convince zealots to pivot 180 degrees and side with you, so you can forget about that from the get-go. But there must be a group of people somewhere along Point A that is persuadable. Otherwise, why bother? And where on the spectrum is your Point B? Where do you realistically think they will wind up? A little ways into the spectrum—say, by writing a letter to their Congressman? Or are you after the far end of the spectrum: storming the gates of the castle?

In basic terms, what *do* you want to do in your piece?

Here is the type of answer you want to be able to provide before you start writing:

> *I want to convince people who use social media without giving too much thought to privacy concerns that we really need to support measures that will crack down on web companies that use our information in sneaky ways they don't tell us about.*

It's a good answer because it identifies an audience. Most likely, these are the new and neutral type of audience we identified in Step 1. It's an issue that many people simply haven't thought about that much, even though they should. The answer specifies the location of Point A (they use social media but don't really think about privacy) and the ideal Point B (supporting some sort of measure to keep web companies from "repurposing" information, such as collecting our purchase data and surreptitiously selling it to spammers). The measure you want them to support might be a piece of legislation, or perhaps you simply want them to be more aware. That's up to you, but you are now not shooting in the dark because you have specified the audience, and figured out how far you think you can move them on the spectrum.

Got it? When you write to persuade, always come up with a one-sentence plan that says, in so many words, I want to move THIS GROUP from THINKING OR DOING *THIS* to THINKING OR DOING *THIS*.

STEP 4: MOVE YOUR READER FROM POINT A TO POINT B ALONG THE PATH OF CONSISTENCY

Academic research shows an astonishing persuasive power attached to the concept of consistency—meaning that humans are attracted to ideas that square with their previous views about things in general and about themselves in particular.

People *love verification that they are right*. Some studies, for example, show that readers looking at car ads pay the most attention to ads for cars they already own. The ad extolling the car they have already bought verifies that they made a good decision, a decision that is consistent with the views about their decision and themselves.

Anyone involved in the persuasive arts should read Robert Cialdini's book *Influence: Science and Practice*. Cialdini, a psychologist, documents among other issues how powerful the concept of consistency is. Among other facets, he explains how modern persuasion theory is based in part on the experiences of brainwashed POWs in the Korean War, some of whom were induced to take a public anti-American stance not by torture or intimidation but by consistency-based persuasion. They were gently coaxed, at first, into admitting that "America is not perfect." From then on, anti-American sentiment became a *matter of degree*. Their statements, recorded and used for propaganda, became increasingly strident and apparently often genuine because they were espousing views *consistent with their first admission*: that America is not perfect.

In persuasion, the working theory of consistency is essentially a restatement of the old phrase, "in for a penny, in for a pound," meaning that once you make a small commitment you are inevitably opening the door to larger commitments. Those commitments will come easily because they are consistent with earlier beliefs and reinforce our idea that we are consistent decision makers.

You certainly have noticed how good salespeople use persuasive techniques to pull you along the path to consistency. Life insurance salespeople want to get you to say "yes," and be consistent right up to the point where you buy a policy. "You care about your family's future, don't you?" (Yes.) Having established that you are someone who cares about family, you are then walked on the path of consistency to the next level. "If something happened to you, you would want to be sure they were taken care of, wouldn't you?" Who on earth would say no? You say yes, and now, you are consistent—a person who cares about the family and wants to take action to protect them. You know how this chain often ends—with a substantial purchase.

To refer back to an earlier statement, *you cannot persuade through an appeal to commitment and consistency if you tell the readers they are wrong*. Would you buy life insurance from someone who said, "You don't have life insurance? You're a damned fool. I'm going to show you the error of your ways. Get out your checkbook."

Moral of the story: Get your readers saying "yes" at the beginning. Make it clear that you and the reader are both intelligent people who are in general agreement with each other on the big points and make the reader "one of us" who will move from Point A to Point B.

STEP 5: ESTABLISH YOUR CREDIBILITY QUICKLY

You're probably familiar with psychology experiments in which people begin jaywalking after they see an older, well-dressed man cross against the light—even though they initially stay put when a young man in jeans crosses the road against the light. And you have likely heard of the infamous Milgram experiments, in which an authoritative man in a lab coat induced students to torture people with electric shock. The shocks weren't real—the person receiving the shocks was an actor planted as part of the experiment—but the subjects didn't know that. Many of them kept delivering what they thought were real electrical jolts until the screaming actor pretended to lose consciousness.

The factors establishing credibility are complicated, but in general we are inclined to commit to people who communicate authoritatively, possess specific training or credentials, or have personal experience with the issue at hand.

Playing the personal experience card is a versatile way to add credibility to your argument, and it works even if you don't have any other credential.

Whatever your claim to authority, work it in near the top of your letter, report, or article. You don't have to be arrogant and certainly don't want to be; just state your case in a reasonable way and inform your reader why your opinion might be worth considering.

Here's an example. With coauthor Phil Benoit, I wrote an op-ed (a type of opinion piece that gets its name from typically being opposite the editorial page) in the *Chronicle of Higher Education*. It defended a ruling in a court case that cracked down on unauthorized use of authors' work by a company that copied portions of books and put them in "course packets."

Our Point A to Point B strategy was this: *We want people, particularly college professors, to give some thought to the idea that using somebody's writing without paying for it is like theft—so the next time they photocopy a book chapter, they realize that it's appropriating material that took a great deal of effort to create.*

Here is how we opened the piece, playing the credibility card right at the top:

> *As textbook authors, we are pleased by the New York District Court's recent decision against Kinko's Graphics Corporation, but we think it is important to clarify why we view the appropriation of our works without permission and payment of fees less as a question of economics and more as an issue of simple decency.*
>
> *Between us, we have written nine college textbooks and several mass-market books. Recently, one of our publishers was among several that sued Kinko's; the judge in that case ruled that Kinko's had infringed on the publishers' copyrights by reproducing, at the direction of college and university faculty members, portions of various books that Kinko's then sold to students as anthologies.*

> One of the first salvos fired in the battle against the unauthorized use of copyrighted material in custom-produced anthologies involved one of our textbooks, Modern Radio Production, *published by Wadsworth Publishing Company.*[1]

We are not publishing giants and we are not legal experts. But we establish at the top that we know what we're talking about because we've been involved in the controversy.

STEP 6: ASSEMBLE EVOCATIVE EVIDENCE AND ARGUMENTS

I realize the idea that you will use evidence and arguments seems obvious but there is a lot more to the process than you might suspect.

First, be aware that there is a considerable amount of research showing that in some cases, facts are not the most persuasive part of an argument and in fact may not even matter. I'm serious. You can lard your document with statistics and studies and still not be particularly convincing. Facts and studies and statistics can be useful in bolstering support among those who already agree with you, *but facts alone won't change hearts and minds.*

I'm not advising you to shun factuality when putting together a piece of persuasive writing. What I'm saying is that if you think you have the facts on your side and therefore will make your case by default with a huge data dump, think again.

An avalanche of facts and numbers is numbing and counterproductive. Choose statistics wisely, *use them judiciously, and make them meaningful,* using the strategies discussed in Chapter 6, Step 6. Be sure you harvest them from reliable sources and cite those sources where necessary.

Instead of data dumps, *deploy a range of examples.* Examples often take the form of stories, and stories feed into that part of the reader's brain that is hard-wired to engage with a narrative.

Quotes are excellent tools for presenting evidence. *A good quote from an expert is a triple treat in persuasive writing:* It packages persuasive information for you, it generally does so in an appealing way (or else you wouldn't be quoting the person's statement), and the authority of the speaker you are quoting rubs off on you.

Use evidence that tells the story in such a way that that reader is likely to say: "I didn't think of that." You are not likely to strong-arm a reader into an opinion. You can, though, very effectively present information they might not have considered and would not be expected to know. It's a fine distinction, but an important one. Don't try to bully with an overload of information. Coax with persuasive facts that give the inside story and appeal to the reader's common sense or conception of fair play. (You may argue that the particular reader has no common sense or conception of fair play, and you may in many cases be right, but everyone *thinks* they have common sense.)

For example, here is how Phil Benoit and I constructed the final argument in the piece described in Step 5—our call to support measures that protect copyright:

> . . . *The appropriation of material that consumed substantial amounts of our time, energy, and resources is, in our minds, tantamount to theft.*
>
> *Strong language? Perhaps, but anyone who has written a textbook realizes that the work is tedious, demanding, and not always particularly rewarding. Scholarly credentials are generally built on research-based publication. While textbooks sometimes do produce substantial royalties, that cannot be taken as a given. Advances are typically small in comparison with those offered by publishers to authors of trade books, and a textbook may not earn anything beyond the advance (much of which may be consumed by the authors' expenses for photography, photocopying, travel, and research activities). In essence, a textbook is a crapshoot with about six months to a year of your working life at stake—and the only real reward, other than personal satisfaction, is monetary.*
>
> *As a result, the idea that material can be reproduced in any form that anyone desires, without so much as notification of the authors and publishers, seems arrogantly exploitative.*[2]

The strategy was to introduce persuasive facts that would draw the reader into our point of view, nuggets that the reader would ostensibly not have known, arguments that would appeal to common sense and fair play, and an emotional appeal that could rise above the sound of the violins I'm sure you heard in the background as you read our complaint.

I'll give you a minute to compose yourself before moving on to the next step.

STEP 7: ACKNOWLEDGE AND COUNTER CONFLICTING ARGUMENTS

Ignoring the fact that there are competing arguments weakens your case because the reader will rightly be suspicious of cards that come from a stacked deck.

You need to acknowledge that there are conflicting views. Sometimes it's implicit, such as my admission in the copyright op-ed that some readers might think I am over the top. I did it by asking a question: "Strong language? [Acknowledgment] Perhaps, but . . ." [Counter]

Sometimes you will want to specifically cite an objection before you counter it.

> *Senator Smith called this proposal "reckless, partisan, and something totally out of the mainstream." [Acknowledgment] I might point out that what we propose is virtually identical to a measure narrowly defeated by the Senate ten years ago—with seven members of Senator Smith's party voting in favor of it. [Counter]*

Be careful with the tone of your acknowledgment and counter. It's OK to be dismissive if that approach is in keeping with the sensibilities of the audience—if, for example, you are writing to reinforce an opinion with a group of readers mostly on your side. But adopt a less confrontational tone, and deflect and restate objections, when writing to a more skeptical audience.

STEP 8: WHEN POSSIBLE, INCLUDE GRAPHICS THAT SUPPORT YOUR CASE

"Graphics" refers to a wide range of components in writing, but for our purposes we'll use the word to mean photos, charts, and illustrations.

Graphics are powerful persuaders because we are conditioned to believe what we see. Therefore, a chart reinforcing whatever notion we are trying to get across has a "scientific" and accurate feel to it.

Also, graphics can get our point across much more quickly and vividly than words. A relevant example is when I was discussing misleading graphics in Chapter 6, Step 7, where I discussed dishonest graphs. Without an illustration, I'm not sure I could have gotten the point across, at least in a fashion that wouldn't put you to sleep.

> *If the left hand access is compressed or truncated, it compresses the range of the results and causes the inaccurate visual perception that the perception rate of growth being skewed and . . .*

Descriptions such as that soon wind up sounding in the mind of the reader like the adults talking in the Charlie Brown cartoons: *wah, wah, wah . . .*

Don't ever use a deceptive graphic, but if appropriate do consider using charts and illustrations that crisply and honestly visualize the point you are trying to make. I could volley statistics at you to demonstrate that retention and persuasion levels are increased via the use of graphics, but I can more easily make my case by asking you to think back to the last high-profile trial you saw televised. I'll bet there was a graphic involved somewhere—a chart, a timeline of events, a depiction of a crime scene. Lawyers, who are obviously in the business of persuasion, invest a great deal of time and money in preparation of graphics. Do a Google search on "trial graphics" and you'll not only see what I mean but will get a first-class visual tour and demonstration of excellent persuasive and informative graphic techniques.

STEP 9: HARNESS FEELINGS, EMOTIONS, AND NARRATIVES TO REINFORCE YOUR ARGUMENTS

Author Maya Angelou summed it up best: "At the end of the day people won't remember what you said or did, they will remember how you made them feel."

You cannot persuade most people through fact and logic alone. There are scores of people who have been in situations where persuasion was critical and assumed that "the facts will speak for themselves." You can locate many of those people in unemployment lines or jail cells.

It is imperative to give voice to your facts, and that involves *relating them to human emotions*—and that process usually involves telling a story.

Brian Clark, the founder of *Copyblogger*, provides a perfect illustration. I've seen this cited for years: what is regarded by many as the most successful sales letter ever written.

It brought in $2 billion for the *Wall Street Journal* and has been used as a model for countless other direct-mail pieces.

The letter connects feelings we all share about success in life, appeals to emotions, particularly fear of failure, and most importantly does so by *telling a story* that keeps us reading.

Here is the opening:

Dear Reader:

On a beautiful late spring afternoon, twenty-five years ago, two young men graduated from the same college. They were very much alike, these two young men. Both had been better than average students, both were personable and both—as young college graduates are—were filled with ambitious dreams for the future.

Recently, these two men returned to college for their 25th reunion.

They were still very much alike. Both were happily married. Both had three children. And both, it turned out, had gone to work for the same Mid-western manufacturing company after graduation, and were still there.

But there was a difference. One of the men was manager of a small department of that company. The other was its president.

What Made The Difference

Have you ever wondered, as I have, what makes this kind of difference in people's lives? It isn't always a native intelligence or talent or dedication. It isn't that one person wants success and the other doesn't.

The difference lies in what each person knows and how he or she makes use of that knowledge.

And that is why I am writing to you and to people like you about the Wall Street Journal. *For that is the whole purpose of the* Journal: *To give its readers knowledge—knowledge that they can use in business. . . .*[3]

STEP 10: PROVIDE A CONCLUSION THAT FUNNELS THE READERS' VIEWS INTO THE CONCLUSION YOU WANT THEM TO DRAW

The most important part of a sales pitch is asking for the sale. It's not uncommon for neophyte salespeople to go through a fact-laden pitch but not make an affirmative effort to close the deal.

As a persuasive writer, you *have to close the deal*. You're not asking for money (usually), but you do want to implicitly lead the reader to a conclusion and be clear about what that conclusion is.

If you *are* asking for money—say, in a direct-mail piece—it's essential that you provide a mechanism, or at least some type of clear instruction, at the end of the piece.

I acknowledge that it seems absurd that a writer would leave the reader hanging at the end of a persuasive piece but it happens constantly. Sometimes, we apparently believe that we have done such a thorough job of assembling "facts that speak for themselves" that it's not necessary to punctuate our piece with a conclusion.

Never leave readers hanging! They may still disagree with you at the end, but if you leave the piece essentially unfinished not only will they disagree but they will feel subtly cheated—as though you have wasted their time (which you have).

Draw your readers through the piece and funnel them to a conclusion. By funnel, I mean to use your evidence and anecdotes to narrow the argument down to a conclusion—a central thought with which you want the reader to agree.

For example, in 2012 I wrote a piece advocating more careful and ethical use of personal information collected by Facebook. It began with a general statement setting the stage:

> *As Facebook readies itself to become a publicly traded corporation, it faces the prospect of unrelenting pressure to turn a quarterly profit. At the same time, it confronts close scrutiny from privacy groups and politicians over how it uses the massive troves of data that it collects from its 845 million users. . . .*

A few paragraphs later, after the premise was broadly introduced, I continued the argumentation and provided an example of how the problem has always existed but is magnified by technology:

> *Repurposed information always made us a little uneasy, even before the widespread availability of computer databases. When I volunteered at a museum in the early 1980s, I was surprised to learn that the museum sold its member list to companies that were advertising products that, for whatever reason, were deemed to be attractive to museum members. (I learned this from an angry member who had deduced the source of some unwanted sales calls.) The museum also sold its list to other museums, apparently because a member of one is more likely to be sold on a membership to another.*
>
> *The member's complaint, I thought, was valid. Paraphrased: I joined a museum. I didn't sign up to have my name and address sold to salespeople. I do, though, remember a verbatim quote from his harangue: "I want to deal with people I can trust."*[4]

I provided a few paragraphs of history, showed how modern-day repurposing of information has become, in my view, much more intrusive, and then moved in for the close, which echoed a line used in the middle of the column:

> *Companies trading in personal information, particularly Facebook, have subscribed for too long to the old maxim that it's easier to apologize than to ask permission. Virtually every week we see stories (many of them covered in the pages of this publication) about major online firms that have been forced, usually under the threat of legislation, legal action, or consumer outrage) to back away from some subterranean overreaching centered on user information.*
>
> *So while I hope I don't have my electronic tentacles cut by regulation and while I hope that I don't have to seriously consider cutting back or ending altogether my activities on various Google services or in social media, either is a possibility.*
>
> *I just want to deal with people I can trust.*[5]

Chapter 8

Show, Don't Tell—Master the Technique at the Heart of Compelling Writing

I'm concluding the book with two master classes and some career advice.

In this chapter, we'll look at the advanced technique of getting out of the way and letting the material tell itself. This skill is what moves good writing into the category of great writing.

The next chapter is a master class in using quotes. Good quotes are the secret sauce that gives writing its zest. Both techniques—showing and not telling and using quotes—are intertwined.

STEP 1: LET THE STORY TELL ITSELF WITHOUT TELLING THE READER THE STORY

I can usually identify professional-quality writing within a matter of seconds, and the most immediate tell-tale is whether the writer is helping the story unfold or is clumsily relaying events secondhand.

This is amateurish:

That part of the city is really poor. Children entering kindergarten don't get enough to eat, and you know that you can't concentrate when you're hungry.

Around that part of the city the homes are dysfunctional so of course there isn't any regular schedule of meals, and that is something I heard from students, some of them not having any idea when people usually eat.

This is professional:

Emily's teacher had noticed that the five-year-old had great difficulty concentrating and suspected that she had not eaten before coming in for the afternoon kindergarten session.
The teacher asked what Emily usually had for lunch.
Emily was bewildered: "What's lunch?"

The second example tells a story, has dialogue, and has a punch line at the end. It shows, rather than tells—and it accomplishes the task by using an anecdote.

STEP 2: USE THE STORY THAT TELLS THE STORY: THE POWER OF ANECDOTES

In writing parlance, an anecdote is a story that illustrates a larger issue, and informs the reader more compactly and powerfully than plain, extended exposition. Compelling anecdotes are a favorite technique of pro writers.

This doesn't mean that every anecdote is a good anecdote. *It has to be the story that tells a larger story*—in the case of Step 1, demonstrating with a real-life example that the little girl's home life was such a shambles that not only did she not get lunch, but she also never heard of the concept.

Here are two descriptions of anecdotes that are stories that more effectively tell the larger story. I've chosen to describe the anecdotes rather than reprinting them in their entirety so you can see at a glance what I mean by the "story that tells the story."

Anecdote #1

The Story: The *Wall Street Journal* carried a long and detailed report on how the tradition-bound U.S. Navy often wastes manpower by clinging to hidebound ways of doing things, such as having sailors scrub decks with steel wool when modern machinery can accomplish the job much more efficiently.

The Anecdote: According to the report, an admiral went on a campaign to eradicate such wasteful practices and gave speeches onboard various ships.

One captain said he was captivated by the speech and would put the suggestions into practice. Later, he put the admiral up in the best quarters on the ship, and stationed an enlisted man outside the admiral's quarters in case he needed anything in the middle of the night. The admiral remarked that he had not needed something in the middle of the night that he could not get for himself since he was eleven.

Why the Anecdote Is the Story That Tells the Larger Story: It shows the basic tone-deafness of the captain. He *said* he understood and embraced the concept of not wasting manpower—but was so uncomprehending of his own habits that he squandered an entire night of an enlisted man's duty to take care of a full-grown admiral. The anecdote shows how the trappings of tradition can cloak perception.

Anecdote #2

The Story: I once wrote a long biographical piece about George Eastman, the founder of Kodak and a pioneer in the development of roll film and portable cameras. One aspect of the story was the fact Eastman was incredibly awkward in social situations, even though he desperately wanted companionship (especially that of young women). Eastman used his astonishingly dogged approach to solving problems to create an environment that would meet his needs.

The Anecdote: Eastman would pay for his youngest employees to accompany him on long ocean voyages—but insisted they bring their wives along. Eastman would (I am not making this up) read and study magazines of the day that were probably equivalent to *Seventeen* or *Teen Beat* today so that he could carry on conversations with the girls.

Why the Anecdote Is the Story That Tells the Larger Story: While Eastman's actions sound more like those of a creeper than an inventor, the anecdote illustrates two points that were vital to the story: (1) that Eastman succeeded and in fact became quite a humanitarian despite being a very strange man, and (2) he applied his methodical nature to industry, which wasn't very methodical back then (quality control, for example, was unheard of) and essentially invented the modern method of doing business.

(The Eastman story is reprinted in Chapter 11.)

The takeaway from this discussion is that anecdotes grab readers' attention and frame the issue. But the successful anecdote is one that illustrates an over-arching concept in your story, report, memo, or whatever you are writing. Use anecdotes liberally. *The human mind feeds on stories, not facts.*

STEP 3: USE QUOTES FROM OTHERS TO CONSCRIPT THEM INTO DOING YOUR SHOWING FOR YOU

A "quote" generally means exact wording from one person used word-for-word and is indicated by "quotation marks," which as you remember are used only for defining figures of speech and for indicating exact appropriation of words, and "not" for "emphasis" or "decoration." Got it?

Anyway, a quote can have two forms in most types of writing: a quote that is used as a stand-alone exhibit to illustrate something . . .

> *It's comforting to have people agree with you, but it's also worth remembering that holding a prevalent, unchallenged view comes with risks. As Mark Twain noted, "Whenever you find yourself on the side of the majority, it's time to pause and reflect."*

Or, a quote can be used to indicate words directly relating to the topic being written about. Often the quote is something the writer obtained in person.

> *"I know that it's unpleasant to hear customer complaints," said Sarah Johnston, vice president for corporate planning. "But a complaint is the firm's most valuable form of intelligence and market research."*

In either incarnation quotes lend variety, rhythm, authenticity, and color, and should be used liberally. The graceful inclusion of quotes is a hallmark of professional writing, and the following chapter is entirely devoted to techniques for using quotes effectively.

STEP 4: USE DIALOGUE TO INVOKE REALITY IN THE THEATER OF THE MIND

For our purposes, dialogue basically means an interplay, a conversation among two or more people.

We like dialogue for several reasons. It breaks up the written page, giving the eye a break. Dialogue adds reality to what you write because it imports real words instead of secondhand relaying of information. Perhaps most importantly, dialogue is the universal condiment of writing: It adds flavor, uniqueness, and zing.

It's not always possible to appropriately use dialogue. But when appropriate, use it.

Dialogue is more commonly used in fiction than in fact-based pieces. But it certainly does have a role in nonfiction.

For example, here is weak description and scene from a feature story:

> *Barney is the sage, the father figure for the fire company. But he is not immune to the good-natured but sharp banter that lightens the tense atmosphere as the rescue truck speeds toward a fire. Barney even quoted Shakespeare, which drew some ribbing from the younger men.*

Here is how dialogue sharpens it:

> *Barney is the sage, the father figure for the fire company, and it's not unusual for him to break the inevitable tension with a monologue as the rescue van speeds toward the third fire in their shift.*
>
> *"Don't wimp out when we get there," he said, grabbing onto a rail for support as the truck lurched around a sharp corner. "What's the worst that could happen? Remember, what Shakespeare said: 'Cowards die many times before their deaths.'"*
>
> *"Never thought I'd hear a fireman quoting Shakespeare," the Lieutenant said, shaking his head.*
>
> *A heavyset fireman with a walrus mustache spoke up from the back of the van, shouting over the wail of the siren.*
>
> *"If Shakespeare knew Barney was going to quote it," he said, "he never would a wrote it."*

Dialog, detail, and action all make the writing come to life. You'll note these devices employed in the preceding dialogue:

- It is interrupted by action. Dialogue can become tedious if not punctuated, so add something happening between stretches of talk.
- It is largely free from adverbs. Instead of writing, "the lieutenant said ruefully," use the *action* of him shaking his head. If you must use an adverb, "ruefully" is not a bad choice, but avoid anything bland and commonplace, such as "wittily."
- It captures vernacular. The fireman's words reflected the way he really talked ("would a wrote"), lending authenticity. You have to be careful with quoting people in vernacular or dialect, because if it's overdone it looks as though you are taking a cheap shot. (See Chapter 9, Step 9.)

STEP 5: SHOW EXAMPLES UNFOLDING AND THEN INTRODUCE YOUR PREMISE

Opening a piece with a series of anecdotes or (less often) quotes is a standard way to capture the reader's attention and build up a sense of curiosity—in other words, compelling the reader to wait for the punch line. The punch line is what your piece is about.

Here's an example from the opening of a *TIME* magazine story:

> *If you could walk past the teachers' lounge and listen in, what sorts of stories would you hear? An Iowa high school counselor gets a call from a parent protesting the C her child received on an assignment. "The parent argued every point in the essay," recalls the counselor, who soon realized why the mother was so upset about the grade. "It became apparent that she'd written it."*
>
> *A sixth-grade teacher in California tells a girl in her class that she needs to work on her reading at home, not just in school. "Her mom came in the next day," the teacher says, "and started yelling at me that I had emotionally upset her child."*
>
> *A science teacher in Baltimore, Md., was offering lessons in anatomy when one of the boys in class declared, "There's one less rib in a man than in a woman." The teacher pulled out two skeletons—one male, the other female—and asked the student to count the ribs in each. "The next day," the teacher recalls, "the boy claimed he told his priest what happened and his priest said I was a heretic."[1]*

After another example, the premise of the story is introduced: that there is an ongoing tension between parents who go overboard in their quest for their children's success, and the teachers who have to deal with pushy moms and dads.

Opening with a series of anecdotes that *show* is an excellent technique, applicable to almost any type of writing. Just be sure the anecdote is interesting and tells the larger story.

STEP 6: STAGE SCENES, A TECHNIQUE SURPRISINGLY APPROPRIATE IN MANY TYPES OF WRITING

A scene is something happening, generally in a short, self-contained episode. There is usually action and something significant happens. In the fire truck example in Step 4, the dialogue is set in the context of the vehicle racing to a fire and lurching around a corner.

A scene doesn't have to be high drama, and can be inserted into all sorts of pieces, even business writing. You can replace this:

> *The inspector came and looked at the damage on the factory floor after the fire. He was very observant and took a long time.*

With this:

The inspector stopped in the middle of the factory floor. He surveyed the scene with a 180-degree rotation of his head. Then, did an about face and repeated the process.

Note the word "surveyed." It's a powerful verb and the perfect choice for the scenario. Note, too, the level of detail and inclusion of actions that *show* instead of *tell*.

STEP 7: PROPEL YOUR NARRATIVE WITH A VARIED TAPESTRY OF PEOPLE DOING THINGS AND EVENTS UNFOLDING

Use the methods described in Chapter 6, Steps 1–6 to weave a cohesive story with forward motion. When I say "story," I don't mean fiction: I refer to the action of real life re-created in your writing. Some people say that good nonfiction writing uses techniques of fiction, but you can easily turn that around and say that fiction borrows the techniques of nonfiction because nonfiction is a chronicle of life and fiction reflects reality.

In any event, the goal is to drop in the show-don't-tell techniques in a way that keeps the motion going.

The secret is to mix up the techniques and don't rely too heavily on one. A long series of quotes passed off as an article or report looks exactly like an unconvincing series of quotes passed off as an article or report. That type of strategy not only won't bring energy to your piece but will also suck the life out of it.

Likewise, don't try to put together something that is merely a collection of stories. Bad writers try that because they don't know any better, and editors have actually developed a pejorative name for that approach: a "string of pearls" article.

A little description goes a long way. Describe vividly, but when in doubt about how much is too much, ration your best description to these types of applications:

- Things that are part of the action and help tell the story.

  He pulled up to the crime scene in a city-issued brown sedan that was coated in a layer of grime and bristled with five antennas.

- People who may be confused with other people in the narrative. It's virtually a cosmic, supernatural certainty that you will be cursed by two or more people in your piece having similar names. So distinguish Johnson from Johansen by giving Johnson a descriptive "tag." The image will be fixed in the reader's mind.

Johnson, the budget director, doesn't look like anyone's conception of the guy who keeps the books for the state: He's tall, lanky, and wears cowboy boots and jeans to the office.

- Place settings that are important to the thrust of the story. Here's how P. J. O'Rourke set the scene for a piece about Manila:

Manila today looks like some Ancient Mariner who has lived through it all. The boulevards are tattered and grim and overhung with a dirty hairnet of electrical and phone wires. The standard-issue third-word concrete buildings are stained dead-meat gray by the emphysematous air pollution. Street lighting is haphazard. Ditto for street cleaning. The streets themselves are filled with great big holes. Fires seemed to be frequent. Visits from the fire department less so. There are numerous burned-out buildings. . . .[2]

STEP 8: PLACE ALL OF YOUR NARRATIVE ON A CLEAR TIME LINE

When you are writing about something that unfolds over time, it's jarring to the reader if there is no sense of what took place when. A narrative without time cues becomes a bland goulash of random events.

The human mind craves structure, which is pretty much why we invented clocks and calendars.

You don't have to overdo your timeline, and you don't even have to use actual times or dates if they are not necessary to the piece. Just add hints so that the reader can be oriented in the flow of time:

> *. . . the level of detail was staggering, and he found, to his surprise, that he'd spend the entire morning preparing for the press conference.*
> *. . . after lunch, we met with the sales team.*
> *. . . when Christmas approached, the committee was still no closer to finding a candidate.*

STEP 9: SUBTLY DEMONSTRATE WHY YOUR QUOTES, ANECDOTES, AND DESCRIPTIONS ARE IMPORTANT—AND USE THEM AS A TELLING DETAIL

The elements you use to create life in your piece should generally serve a larger purpose. Now, you have a lot of latitude here: A perfectly valid "larger purpose" is to show that a place is grimy and run-down, or simply to paint a picture of what's happening by describing someone.

But there are telling details that can add meaning to your work. You should include them. You should also include some context, background, or subtle hint about why the detail is important. Set the stage, and use your good quote, description, or anecdote to drive the point home. Think about what you need to communicate, work it into your piece, and then punctuate that idea with a telling detail.

For example:

What you need to subtly communicate to the reader: That a bureaucrat is officious and not entirely concerned with serving the public.

The telling detail: *He smiles only for a second and then drops his expression immediately—never showing his teeth.*

What you need to subtly communicate to the reader: The city's police department is out of touch, going through the motions, pretty much doing their job by the numbers.

The telling detail: A reporter is assigned to a ride-along with a beat cop. The cop takes the car through a car wash with a reporter inside, and asks the reporter to hold a newspaper up to the window because it doesn't shut properly and the water will squirt in. The cop tells the reporter: "The chief says any car is supposed to be washed if a civilian is going on a ride-along."

STEP 10: USE YOUR MOST VIVID DETAILS AND EVOCATIVE DESCRIPTIONS WHEN YOU MAKE YOUR "SHOW POINT"

I'll close this section with an excellent technique that is easy to employ but easy to overlook. Don't forget to include one or more "show points."

Every piece of writing has a premise, the essential idea you want to communicate. If it doesn't have a central idea, there's little point in writing it and less point in reading it.

The entire piece should explore and back up the premise, but it's always effective to have a climactic point where detail and action illustrate the premise powerfully, usually in some sort of scene.

The show point, as I call it, doesn't have to be at the end. About two-thirds of the way through the piece is a good location, although you can pretty much put it anywhere.

Reinforce your show point with as many "show" details as you can reasonably orchestrate. *Draw out the telling detail. Focus on the most powerful story that tells the story.*

I've referred to George Orwell's "A Hanging" previously in this book and have included it in Chapter 11. It's an outstanding piece of writing, and is widely available on the web should you wish to read the whole thing, which I hope you do. "A Hanging" was about an execution Orwell may have witnessed as a young police officer stationed in India. (Whether it was about one actual event is unclear.) He found the process bizarre and brutal, but rather than *telling* the reader his opinions he *showed* what, for him, was the incongruity of killing a healthy, conscious person.

Note the prolonged description that reinforces the viability of the soon-to-be dead man, and the famous show point, a little more than halfway through the essay: when the condemned man steps around a puddle.

> *It was about forty yards to the gallows. I watched the bare brown back of the prisoner marching in front of me. He walked clumsily with his bound arms, but quite steadily, with that bobbing gait of the Indian who never straightens his knees. At each step his muscles slid neatly into place, the lock of hair on his scalp danced up and down, his feet printed themselves on the wet gravel. And once, in spite of the men who gripped him by each shoulder, he stepped slightly aside to avoid a puddle on the path.*
>
> *It is curious, but till that moment I had never realized what it means to destroy a healthy, conscious man. When I saw the prisoner step aside to avoid the puddle, I saw the mystery, the unspeakable wrongness, of cutting a life short when it is in full tide. This man was not dying, he was alive just as we were alive. All the organs of his body were working—bowels digesting food, skin renewing itself, nails growing, tissues forming—all toiling away in solemn foolery.*[3]

Chapter 9

Borrow from the Best: Use Quotes to Add Power to Your Writing

Why use quotes in your writing?

Would you rather spend the next two hours watching a play or a mime?

The prosecution rests.

STEP 1: UNDERSTAND WHY CHURCHILL SAID, "QUOTATIONS, ENGRAVED UPON THE MEMORY, GIVE YOU GOOD THOUGHTS"

Churchill liked to read books of quotations, and urged others to do likewise. I concur with his advice, especially in the sense that I suspect he meant it. By reading collections of quotations, and not just hunting for one that meets your immediate needs, you absorb, through osmosis, a broad spectrum of eloquence.

As discussed briefly in Chapter 8, Step 3, there are two types of quotes: The first is those that are taken as gems of brilliance expression, such as the Churchill quote earlier. For the sake of discussion, let's call them "gem quotes." The second type is those used journalistically to add explanation and color. Journalistic quotes can be gathered during an interview or taken from other sources as long as they are properly attributed.

Either way, using quotes lends power, authenticity, and expressiveness to your writing. Wielding quotes properly is a relatively advanced technique, which is why I am covering it as the last lesson in the mechanics of writing.

STEP 2: USE A QUOTE WHEN YOU CAN'T SAY IT PERFECTLY BUT SOMEONE ELSE ALREADY HAS

Why bother spending a lot of time crafting something that is creaky and limps along like this:

> *Yes, I am switching parties, but I reject the accusation that I am a flip-flopper—as though there is something bad about re-aligning myself with a party that more closely reflects how my views have evolved.*

When you can channel Churchill with a gem quote:

> *Let me respond to that by quoting Churchill: "Some men change their party for the sake of their principles; others their principles for the sake of their party."*

Why be pedestrian and lukewarm when trying to inspire:

> *We really need to keep working on this project. I know we haven't hit on the right answer yet, but that doesn't mean we should stop trying.*

When you can echo Edison and make your point with precision and power:

> *Giving up is the easy way out. Thomas Edison realized that. He predicted that "the most certain way to succeed is always to try just one more time."*

The options are limitless. In addition to infinite cat videos, the Internet is a portal for millions of quotes. Just search on the subject, such as "quotes on betrayal," "quotes about success," "inspiring quotes." It's always a good idea to cross-check a couple of sites to make sure the quote is properly attributed. It's not unusual for some quotes to variously be attributed to two people—say, Will Rogers and Mark Twain—so you need to research and go with what in your judgment is a reliable source. Some quotes are falsely attributed, often when political messages are paired with a celebrity, so be careful.

STEP 3: USE QUOTES TO LEND AUTHORITY

Facts and statistics have limited value in persuasive and informative writing for three reasons: (1) people mistrust many statistics, (2) most readers know that facts can be manipulated in such a way as to tell a lie, and (3) a repetitive drumbeat of facts can be numbing.

This doesn't mean you should ignore facts. Just remember, as stated before, facts do not speak for themselves. As the great Roman orator Cicero noted, "[I]f truth were self-evident, eloquence would not be necessary."

Conveniently, that's an example of using a gem quote to strengthen your case by lending authority. You can also utilize journalistic quotes to lend authority to your writing, along with perspective and readability.

Compare:

> *We can enter into this deal confident that the economy will rebound. I have read many reports, including government predictions, and they almost all indicate to me that things will be on the upswing within the next six months.*

With:

> *We can enter into the deal confident that the economy will rebound. "Almost every major indicator points to a major recovery," says Harvard economist Everett Sloane, a former undersecretary of the Treasury. "I've seen these cycles repeat themselves a dozen times, and I'm certain that the markets will be moving up steadily in six months."*

The journalistic quote imparts credibility and includes relevant detail regarding the number of similar cycles the expert has observed. Remember, the first example (*"We can enter into this deal confident that the economy will rebound. I have read many reports. . ."*) touts *your* judgment. The second stresses the judgment of a major economist.

You'll note that virtually every story in every major newspaper or magazines uses quotes from authoritative sources.

Caveat: A writer can unfairly stack quotes as well as stack facts. There is a term for this in the journalism business: "speaking through sources," meaning only interviewing and quoting people you know will make your case. Be careful of this tactic; stacking the deck in persuasive writing is generally acceptable as long as you somehow acknowledge competing opinions, but it's bad form if you are trying to present your work as a legitimate and unbiased effort to inform.

So make every effort to employ honest quotes from experts, or from people who are eyewitnesses or have firsthand experience with the issue about which you're writing.

STEP 4: USE QUOTES TO ADD COLOR

Quotes allow the writer easy access to colorful and figurative language, which is handy because you don't have to bother composing the appealing sentences yourself. All you have to do is harvest them.

For example, here is a reasonably well-written sentence but it's bland:

> Despite the high crime rate in the city's Division Street neighborhood, the streets are alive with hundreds of people at 2 a.m. Sgt. Robert Pine, who has patrolled the district for more than a decade, says that the mix of potential victims and likely predators is volatile.

You can make the statement come alive if the subject is nice enough to give you colorful quote like this one:

> Despite the high crime rate in the city's Division Street neighborhood, the streets are alive with hundreds of people at 2 a.m. "Half the people you see right now are crooks," says Sgt. Robert Pine, who has patrolled this district for more than a decade. "Half are victims. And they're doing their damndest to get together."

STEP 5: USE PARTIAL QUOTES AND PARAPHRASES TO MAKE THE QUOTE MORE READABLE

Unfortunately, you can't always rely on people to provide you with colorful and succinct quotes. In fact, a mark of the amateur is to include an entire quote even if it drones and rambles:

> "The situation requires some immediate remediation," says Robert McElwain, the eastern division director of finance. "There were attempts to restructure the debt in 2011, 2013, and 2014. Three times and no one could come to an agreement. It's something that needs to be solved and we keep putting it off. This could cause catastrophic problems. We can't keep kicking the can down the road."

The solution is to use a *partial quote*. Paraphrase the part of the quote that simply imparts information; only use the good parts, the portions that add color.

> Robert McElwain, the eastern division director of finance, says the debt problem has been brought to the table three times but was never fixed. He predicts "catastrophic problems" if the situation isn't fixed, and warns that "we can't keep kicking the can down the road."

You can quote as much or as little of the actual quote as you want, as long as you paraphrase accurately. Sometimes, you'll only want to use key words:

> *Morton was sharply critical of the hiring process, claiming the preferential treatment given one candidate amounted to a "bag job."*

Here is a summary of the rules for deciding when to paraphrase a quote and how much to paraphrase:

- Paraphrase something that is rambling or uninteresting that could be shortened.
- Paraphrase a complicated explanation that you can summarize more clearly than the speaker did.
- Paraphrase any time you can say it better.
- But do not excessively paraphrase major statements. If the president of the company announces layoffs and provides justification, you are better off using as many exact quotes as possible.

STEP 6: BE TRANSPARENT IN CITING THE SOURCE OF YOUR QUOTES

Lifting a quote that someone else invested a lot of effort into getting is a major transgression in professional writing. Never lift a journalistic quote from another source and imply, intentionally or unintentionally, that you were the one who obtained it.

Feel free to use someone else's quote when you cite the source, like this:

> *"We want mining business to settle in Monroe County," Mayor Hilliard told the* Monroe Herald *in a December, 2015 interview, "and we will put our money where our mouth is by offering generous tax credits."*

You can't appropriate too many quotes, even if you give credit. There is no hard-and-fast rule, but generally you're safe if you stick to a hundred words or fewer if you are writing a several-page piece.

If you conducted the interview, the quote is yours and you can use as much as you want. While it's not essential, it's a good idea to note that the quote came from a personal interview.

> *During an interview I conducted in 2015, Drexler acknowledged "massive headaches" ahead in the project.*

It's also a good idea to indicate if the exchange came through e-mail.

STEP 7: ATTRIBUTE QUOTES ETHICALLY

The process of indicating what quote came from where is called attribution. Professional writers know how to attribute properly, and amateurs often don't.

Improper attribution can be more than cosmetically clumsy: It can sometimes get you into trouble.

In general, you want to attribute the source of a quote or any piece of information if the information is not common knowledge and is in some way questionable or controversial.

Also, if the information is controversial and the time element is important, attribute quotes using the past tense.

And if someone tells you something that you personally did not witness, put it in quotes and cite the person who told you. If you write, *Bob Smith robbed a bank,* and it turns out later that it was a case of mistaken identity and Bob Smith did not rob a bank, you are in bigger trouble than Bob Smith. You are assuming ownership of the now-incorrect claim that Bob Smith robbed a bank. If you write *New York police say Bob Smith robbed a bank*, and it turns out Bob Smith did not rob a bank, you are more or less off the hook, although your statement is technically no longer true because police are no longer "saying" Smith robbed a bank.

If you write *"Bob Smith was charged with the robbery of the First National Bank branch on 32nd St.," said Capt. Robert LeRoy of the 87th precinct*, you are completely off the hook because what you wrote is true, even if the charge later turns out to be false. You are accurately and completely reporting what happened, pinning it in time, and attributing it to someone in a position to have authoritative knowledge of the incident.

STEP 8: ATTRIBUTE QUOTES GRACEFULLY AND GRAMMATICALLY

You can deploy quotes in a professional manner by following these rules:

- For most quotes, put attribution at the end of the sentence. Put a comma inside the quotation mark and attribute with "_____ said."

    "We have had the best quarterly sales figures in the history of the organization," Mary Wilson said.

- Use "said" or "says." The choice of tense is up to you, but if it's a statement that is controversial or about a situation that is fluid, past tense is a better choice. If it's feature-type, human-interest writing, go with present tense. But don't mechanically try to invent alternatives to "said" or "says." Readers are used so accustomed to seeing "said" that they simply won't notice. They *will* notice, however, if you use an awkward attribution.

> *"We have had the best quarterly sales figures in the history of the organization," Mary Wilson exclaimed.*

- Readers will also perceive an editorial slant in the attribution if you get tricky with it. Don't do this, for example, unless you really intend to convey the negative impression it leaves:

> *"We have had the best quarterly sales figures in the history of the organization," Mary Wilson gushed.*

- Put the name first (Wilson said) unless you are further identifying Wilson. If you further identify her with more than a couple words of description, put "said" first.

> *"We have had the best quarterly sales figures in the history of the organization," said Mary Wilson, regional vice president for sales.*

- Put attribution first when you are changing speakers.

> *"We have had the best quarterly sales figures in the history of the organization," said Mary Wilson, regional vice president for sales.*
>
> *But Robert Ellis, the firm's director of accounting, says that "the numbers are deceptive and represent a one-time blip. We shouldn't read too much into them."*

- Capitalize job titles when they come before a name. Leave them lowercase after the name. When you capitalize titles, you are telling the reader you are using the precise, formal title, so be sure you have it right.

> *Yale Professor of Economics Lydon Roberts says the report "isn't worth the paper it's printed on."*
>
> *Lydon Roberts, an economics professor at Yale, says the report "isn't worth the paper it's printed on."*

(Be careful about academic titles. There are all sorts of different formal job titles for professors, including assistant professor and associate professor, so when making a specific identification of a job title, with the title capitalized, it's essential to get it right.)

- If it is a long quote, put the attribution after the first sentence or phrase.

> *"This report isn't worth the paper it's printed on," says Lydon Roberts, an economics professor at Yale. "It makes no distinction between full-time and part-time jobs added last year. That's a huge difference, and without knowing more we have no idea if the economy is getting better or worse."*

- Usually you will put a comma before the introduction of a quote.

> *But Yale's Lydon Roberts says, "This report isn't worth the paper it's printed on."*

- But if you are introducing, in your own words, the first few words of the quote, or are using a couple key words, don't use a comma to introduce the quote.

  But Yale's Lydon Roberts says the report is worthless, and the lack of distinction between full and part-time jobs leaves us with "no idea of whether the economy is better or worse."

  But the report isn't "worth the paper it's printed on," says Yale's Lydon Roberts.

- Capitalize the first word of a quote if the quote is a complete sentence, even if the quoted part starts in the middle of your sentence.

  But Yale's Lydon Roberts says, "This report isn't worth the paper it's printed on."

- You only have to attribute by title once, but if you reintroduce the speaker farther down in the piece, a partial reintroduction is a good reminder. You could just write, "Yale's Roberts" if you re-introduce him five paragraphs later.

STEP 9: CHANGE QUOTES WITH EXTREME CAUTION

Writers are not supposed to change the wording of quotes, although almost every writer has to. In real life, people hem and haw, interject tangential remarks, and make slips of the tongue. Reprinting a rambling quote word-for-word could be considered a way of taking a cheap shot.

Major news organizations take this question seriously because changing a quote can be dangerous business. In general, most news policies say that it is acceptable to fix a quote to eliminate slips of the tongue or other throwaway parts of the quote. But those policies can be almost self-contradictory in that they instruct reporters not to quote someone in dialect, meaning they should not reprint a statement like, "I ain't gonna do that."

Adding to the confusion is the fact that many quotes aren't literal quotes to begin with; reporters have jotted them down in notebooks and have done their best to decode them later in the day when they are writing their stories. Very few American journalists take shorthand (though it's more common in England) so they could not take the quote down word-for-word in real time anyway. Some reporters use audio recorders to capture exact quotes, but many do not. Personally, I don't use a recorder. I've always felt it adds a barrier between the subject and the writer and inhibits the flow of an interview. I am not a particularly speedy or legible note-taker, either.

What I do is to listen carefully and give my best rendition of what the interviewee was saying, keeping as close to my notes as I can. I am less concerned with word-for-word accuracy than of truthfully capturing the spirit and flavor of what was said. And I will note that I have published in the neighborhood of 500 articles and have never once had the accuracy of a quote challenged.

I *have* had people upset when I quoted them in dialect, though. They didn't argue about the veracity of the quote but were angry because I didn't fix it. For example, I once quoted a cop this way: "Nobody trusts nobody after dark."

He thought it was a cheap shot for me to quote him ungrammatically. I had given serious thought to fixing the quote, but the quote was too good, too realistic, for me to change. After all, once I get into the business of fixing interviewees' grammar and sentence construction, where does it end? How far do I go to make them sound smart? "Indubitably, there is a paucity of belief in the veracity of others after sundown?"

Your strategy in handling such situations may vary according to the purpose of your writing and its venue, but my general recommendations are:

- Fix the types of grammatical errors and throwaways we all make in common speech.
- Do not quote someone in dialect (including a pattern of poor grammar) if it is demeaning or there is no legitimate reason to do so. But don't go overboard with fixing grammar. If there is a reason to quote ungrammatically (including a need to reflect the authenticity of the interview) do so, but with caution.

When in doubt, you can always paraphrase.

STEP 10: EMPLOY EVOCATIVE INTERVIEW TECHNIQUES TO COAX A QUOTE FROM A SOURCE

Including genuine, self-harvested quotes in your writing elevates your work to a much higher plane. Having said that, poor quotes are no better than no quotes at all. You have to be able to conduct an interview in a way that elicits interesting answers.

I have developed a ten-point (of course) guide for effective interviewing:

One: Do some background research on the person you are interviewing. This is essential. There's an old saying that there's no such thing as a stupid question. That, frankly, is stupid advice. If you ask a dumb question of an interviewee, something that easily could have been obtained in a quick web search, you are wasting the interviewee's time as well as your own.

Two: Before the interview begins, let the person know what the purpose is and what you are after. People are often needlessly paranoid about interviews, and can be defensive and uncooperative unless put at ease. Try, for example: "I'm doing a story for the company newsletter about trends in intellectual property law and how that might affect us. I wanted to talk with you not only because you're a lawyer in this field, but because I've read that you have pretty strong opinions about how current regulations are ineffective. Can you tell me about . . ."

Three: Put together a list of questions but don't be a slave to the list. Ask follow-ups if the interviewee tells you something interesting; don't just mechanically rattle off the next question.

Four: Follow up with another question when an interviewee blows you off with a pat answer. If you get, "those issues are all addressed in our policy," ask, "could you give me an example?" Asking for an example almost always draws out a reluctant interviewee.

Five: Ask simple, single-part questions. A complex question with multiple parts usually doesn't get a very clear response, plus the awkwardness sometimes irritates the person you are interviewing.

Six: Avoid yes-or-no questions, unless you are trying to pin an evasive interviewee down. Try to initiate a conversation. "What do you think about the current proposal?" is better than, "Do you favor the current proposal?"

Seven: Personalize questions. If you ask, "what is your agency's position on . . ." you may prompt your interviewee to shut down, responding, "I can't speak for the agency." Instead, try "what sort of things do you and your agency do to overcome . . ."

Eight: Be careful of making meaningless noises during the interview. Saying "uh-huh" after every response not only becomes annoying, but it also establishes a rhythm in which the interviewee may wait for you to say "uh-huh" before continuing. Likewise, try not to establish a perceptible rhythm with your note-taking. If you don't write anything down until your interviewee says something that strikes your fancy, the person may assume that you are not paying attention when you are not writing things down. A good solution: write *all the time*, even if you doodle on the page. The interviewee won't know what you are writing, and won't become concerned about what you are writing down and what you are not.

Nine: Sometimes the best question is no question. If a person isn't being responsive, just wait. People hate silence, finding it awkward, and will usually do anything to fill it—including giving you a responsive answer.

Ten: The best tip of all: If your interviewee says, "no comment," ask "why don't you want to comment?" You'll often get the answer you wanted.

Chapter 10

Grow as a Writer Using
This Ten-Step Plan

The purpose of this concluding section is to provide a roadmap for you to follow as you progress as a writer. Remember, the premise of this book is that there is really no such thing as "business writing" any more. In the digitally connected world, the "business writer" is a blogger, commentator, a public relations professional, a journalist who writes about a particular area of expertise in company or general-interest publications, or all of these.

Your professional-level writing skills may lead you to new and unexpected career paths. You might, some day, compile your knowledge into a book. Publishing has fewer barriers to entry in the electronic age, and even traditional publishers are always on the lookout for fresh, authentic, and authoritative works.

Today, writing is an integral part of many professional careers, and the demarcation between a professional who writes and a professional writer is blurry.

With that in mind, what follows is a brief guide to becoming either.

STEP 1: MODEL YOUR STYLE ON YOUR FAVORITES: GOOD WRITING IS THE SINCEREST FORM OF IMITATION

Every writer imitates other writers. Because reading is essential to writing, we all get our grounding in the works of others, starting with Dick and Jane or Grimm's Fairy Tales.

There's a word for when your imitation becomes too obvious: "derivative." It is a derogatory term meaning that you are obviously aping someone else's style and doing it in a second-rate way.

So, don't be derivative. But stop *just short* of being derivative. And if you are going to be derivative, be derivative of a number of good authors whose work speaks to you in some way.

When I teach writing I am open about the authors I have borrowed from. I'll give you a partial list. Perhaps you might take some time and graze snippets of their work; even a brief reading of a paragraph or two of their works somewhere on the Internet can give you an indication of what makes their work so special.

I have modeled parts of my writing style after:

- *George Plimpton*, who was noted for his "participatory journalism." He would inject himself into a story, such as the time he wrote about what it was like to attend a training camp for a professional football team, pretending to be a prospective quarterback. He didn't fool anybody for long, but his sharp, self-deprecating wit brought the reader into the world he'd invaded. No one was better than Plimpton at guiding the reader into the environment of another culture or profession. He dug up the most fascinating anecdotes and created luminous scenes to enthrall the reader.
- *Dave Barry*, who is funny because he is particularly observant about life's absurdities. That's why his humor rings true. He also is a master at timing. It's hard to describe timing, but you'll get what I mean if you read a few of his columns. The biting observations come just at the right time, after precisely the correct setup.
- *Vance Packard*, who popularized sociology. His books were popular when I was a teenager, and for whatever reason I took a liking to his approach, which was this: Identify a compelling issue, look for material about the issue that would shock and surprise the audience, and tell the story using research translated into plain English. His best book, in my opinion, was *A Nation of Strangers*—based on the premise that the change in demographic patterns that dislocated people from traditional communities also changed the way we think and act as a society. He once told me it was his favorite book, too.

You probably already have favorite authors whose work speaks to you for various reasons. Try to define those reasons: What, specifically, draws you to them? How do they produce the effect that pleases you?

Go through their copy, page-by-page, figuratively *eat* their words and phrases, and then make them a part of your own work.

I recommend you read *The Little Book of Talent,* in which author Daniel Coyle compiled the traits that are common among high performers. Among the most telling was the willingness and desire to, shall we say, appropriate . . .

> We are often told that talented people acquire their skill by following their "natural instincts." This sounds nice, but in fact it is baloney. All improvement is about absorbing and applying new information, and the best source of information is top performers. So steal it.
>
> Stealing has a long tradition in art, sports, and design, where it often goes by the name of "influence." The young Steve Jobs stole the idea for the computer mouse and drop-down menus from the Xerox Palo Alto Research Center. The young Beatles stole the high "woooo" sounds in "She Loves You," "From Me to You," and "Twist and Shout" from their idol Little Richard. The young Babe Ruth based his swing on the mighty uppercut of his hero, Shoeless Joe Jackson. As Pablo Picasso (no slouch at theft himself) put it, "Good artists borrow. Great artists steal."[1]

STEP 2: START AN ORGANIZED FILE OF ANECDOTES, QUOTES, AND FACTS THAT ARE OF PARTICULAR USE TO YOU

There's no substitute for having an organized trove of material at your disposal. When you come across something that you suspect will be useful in the future, copy it and file it. The mechanism for filing is a matter of choice, but I will put in a plug for cloud-based storage.

There are programs devoted to taking, keeping, and filing notes, such as Evernote, and for some people they work very well. I favor Google Drive.

Google Drive is a free service offered by Google, and it allows you to access a copious amount of free storage and purchase additional storage if you have large files. You can access your stuff from anywhere that has an Internet connection.

The advantage of Google Drive goes beyond being free; it has the additional advantage of offering easily accessible storage. You also can search all your material for specific words in the content or titles of documents. Google Drive's online word processing program, which looks and acts a lot like Microsoft Word, lets you collaborate with a coauthor in real time. (Yes, you can actually see each other typing as you enter text, regardless of whether your coauthor is in the next room or a distant continent.)

There are many cloud-based storage options, of course, and you may like them better than Google Drive. The important goal is to constantly harvest material that will be of use and store it. I can't emphasize strongly enough the need to store relevant material as you come across it. You may think you'll remember where to find it again, and maybe you will, but maybe you won't. Thirty seconds now can save you half an hour of search time later.

STEP 3: TAKE NOTES ASSIDUOUSLY

At the risk of sounding like an infomercial hustler, I'm going to try to sell you on a product that can genuinely be a life-changer.

And you can get this product for under five dollars.

It's a *notebook*. Get one. Carry it always. End of sentence. Full stop. I mean it.

Thoughts are fleeting, and once they fly away, they can never be coaxed back into the cage. Remember that the idea you capture in your notebook may not *in itself* be earth-shattering, but in conjunction with other thoughts you collect you may generate some collective seismic activity.

A good example of this effect is Beethoven. He didn't write any symphonies in his notebook but he did capture phrases and inflections that flashed through his mind. Later, he would meld them into larger works. Apparently Beethoven took his notebook everywhere; many of the paintings in which he is depicted show him clutching a notebook or writing in it.[2]

The choice of notebook is a personal decision but as someone who has been compelled by profession to carry one for four decades I can offer some advice:

- The best notebook is the one you have with you. Therefore, make it easy to carry. I favor miniscule Moleskine notebooks that actually are so small that they are hard to write on legibly, but are no burden to carry so I can trust myself to always have it with me. While I have at times carried a larger reporter-style notebook, I found it cumbersome. Stuck in my back pocket it protrudes and scratches the back of my car seat, and inserted in a breast pocket it spoils the line of the suit jacket. Those without leather car seats or vanity issues may find them acceptable, however. The standard pocket notebook, 3 by 5 inches, also works.
- Electronic note-taking can be effective but intrusive, so I stick to a notebook. I do have several note-taking applications for my collection of iPads, and I occasionally take notes on my phone (either by typing or

with a stylus). But iPads have the disadvantage of not being omnipresent, and the phone is awkward and intrusive. If an idea comes to you during a conversation, most people are accepting (even flattered) if you retrieve your pocket notebook, but pulling out the smartphone sends a different signal altogether. On occasion I do use the "voice memo" command of my smartphone to make spoken notes while driving or otherwise occupied.

- Make it a habit to transcribe your notes every day. Your scrawlings will lose legibility and personal context after a couple of days, so type them up while they are fresh in your mind. You can overlook the mundane stuff, like shopping lists, but a couple of minutes (and that's really all it takes) to transcribe and save your thoughts in Google Drive file is a small investment with a potentially enormous payback.
- Use your notebook for *everything you keep track of*, and get a new one when you fill it. I put a start date on the inside flap of my current notebook, and when I fill it I add the end date and consign the notebook to a drawer. I use the notebook for pretty much everything except to-do lists, which are better handled in the Google Tasks app of my smartphone. The point of this strategy is that if you keep different notes on different media, you'll lose track of them and won't be inclined to have each and every separate notebook or other note-taking device with you. I have a decade's worth of notes stored away, and I do occasionally find reason to consult them or the transcribed versions on my cloud account.

STEP 4: LEARN WHAT "ASSIDUOUS" MEANS AND SEE HOW KNOWING ONE LATIN ROOT CAN ADD THREE EXCELLENT ENGLISH WORDS TO YOUR REPERTOIRE, AND THEN FORMULATE A LIFETIME VOCABULARY-BUILDING PLAN

I've been waiting to spring this one on you since Chapter 3, Step 7.

"Assiduous" means diligent, showing great devotion in pursuing something. It comes from that same Latin root *sed*, and it basically means "to sit down with your work." As I explained in Chapter 3, Step 7, knowing *sed* can unlock an eclectic family of words, including "sedate," "sedative," and "insidious."

Now, I want to make a heavy-handed point here. If you read Chapter 3, Step 7, even if you read it a month ago, or a *year* ago, I'll bet you still remember "sedate," "sedative," and "insidious." You also remember the precise meaning of the word "ostracize" and the story behind it, don't you? That's because word origins and the derivation of words put vocabulary into a context we can all understand: *stories*.

Learning the stories behind words is part of the method to developing a powerful vocabulary, the tool that will empower you to assemble a precise array of words to power your point. (And the tool that will empower you to say "array" and not "bunch.")

The entire method is this:

- **Look up *every* word when you don't know the meaning or are unsure of the precise connotation.** Doing this will make clear the difference between similar-sounding words, such as "connotation" and "denotation." (Look it up.) Also, you'll develop a sense for the relative intensity of words. For example, you'll know where "jealousy" and "envy" exist along the scale of passion and meaning. The words have slightly different meanings. "Jealousy" usually means resentment or fear that someone will take something of yours, like a girlfriend or boyfriend. "Envy" has only two parties involved instead of three: You envy your neighbor because he won the lottery. There is no third party (a girlfriend who may be lured away) involved. In addition, the word "envy" usually carries a little more intensity than "jealous." It's a stronger word that implies an active resentment or even hatred.
- **When you look up a word, read the section about the derivation as well as the definition.** That way, you'll often (though not always) have a story to go with it, hence a narrative to wire the word into your brain. By the way, "jealous" comes from the Greek word *zelos,* which means "heat." It's the same root as "zealous." "Envy" comes from the Latin *invidia,* which literally means "see into" and came to mean "regard with malice" before evolving into "envy." I know you can't remember all the etymologies—no one can—but these stories can stick with you, and knowing one often opens the door to knowing another. For example, the word "invidious" is a cousin of envy. It is from the same "look into" root and means tending to cause envy or some sort of animosity.
- **Use the word a few times to cement it into your memory.** Try not to be too obvious, but drop it into a conversation, letter, or article. Just be sure it precisely squares with your meaning. Before long, the word will be neatly stored in the verbal arsenal of your brain, waiting to be deployed on an instant's notice.

STEP 5: READ WITH A PURPOSE: GRAZE IN DIFFERENT GENRES—IN A SYSTEMATIC WAY—TO NOURISH OVERALL VERBAL GROWTH

A friend of mine is dyslexic, and for most of his youth he struggled with the confounding contortions of a language filtered through his different mental wiring, which simply wasn't built to process it. Today he is an accomplished artist, quite famous in his specialty, and credits a good part of his success to voracious and omnivorous reading.

He couldn't read well in the normal way, so he started subscribing to a series of audiobooks that were meant for the blind. Later, of course, he was able to listen to readily available audio books on Audible and other sources.

He has read thousands of books, and has absorbed and funneled the ideas of Walt Whitman, James Joyce, and dozens of others into his artistic vision. Such is the power of reading.

You never know what you'll absorb until you make an effort to absorb it. As a writer, you'll sometimes be able to directly employ the turn of a phrase from an author you have read. Sometimes it will be an idea or concept that informs your vision.

There's nothing wrong with reading deeply in an area you like, but try to expand into uncharted, even uncomfortable territory. Make up your own system, whether it's a book per month or per year, in traditional format or audio. Make broadening your horizons your salient goal. (Salient means "most important" or "most notable," and it comes from a Latin word meaning "to leap." I'll stop now.)

STEP 6: TEST YOUR LIMITS BY TRYING DIFFERENT STYLES AND GENRES

Without question the best writing training I ever had was working in radio and TV news and reading my own copy. (Most on-air newspeople write at least some of their copy.) Hearing the words come out of my mouth, or hearing me stumble over the malformed sentences coming out of my mouth, gave me enormous insight into structure, clarity, and rhythm.

You can become a newscaster reaching audiences worldwide. Seriously. You can do it this afternoon. Just start a podcast. Stretch your talents and technical skills a bit. It's not difficult; you can find comprehensive instructions anywhere on the web, along with free software and free places to mount and distribute the podcast.

Should that not appeal to you, you can always simply read your copy aloud. That's not only a good learning method but a great way to spot typos and other errors. And even if that is too much work, have your computer read back your prose.

Try writing fiction and reading books about fiction; doing so will provide insight into crafting scenes and dialogue, skills adaptable to prose writing. Remember, of course, that prose-writing skills are infinitely adaptable to fiction.

I'd recommend that you try writing a play. I wrote a couple of plays and had one produced, and it was awful. Having said that,

I lived through it and eventually lived it down, and listening to actors attempting to chew through my wooden dialogue was a good lesson on how to better craft my quotes in prose.

STEP 7: CREATE AN ENVIRONMENT, SCHEDULE, AND SYSTEM THAT SUPPORT YOUR WRITING GOALS

I am going to shift back into infomercial mode and sell you on a concept that is almost as life-changing as carrying a notebook.

Here is my pitch: If you write on a professional writer's schedule you can drastically increase your productivity and effectiveness.

I am aware that very competent and sometimes brilliant writers have oddball schedules that work for them, and there is no point in arguing with success. But I've made something of a study of writing habits, and firmly believe in these recommendations:

- Put yourself on a regular quota. Four or five double-spaced pages a day is a good target. Even one page a day is better than nothing. One page a day can translate to a book a year. Schedule work time. Clearly, the demands of your job may take scheduling out of your control, but you can find time if you really want to. The problem with waiting for inspiration is that it may never come. And, as artist Chuck Close noted, "Inspiration is for amateurs. I just get to work."
- Give yourself a daily quota. The utility of a writing quota is that you don't give yourself an out; you have to produce the four pages or wither to a skeleton in your chair. But there is a carrot as well as a stick: When you finish the four pages, you're done. Turn off the computer or go to YouTube and watch cat videos or do whatever you like. I try not to keep going after reaching my quota even when I want to, even when I'm on a roll. If you stop when you look forward to continuing, you are more likely to actually continue the next day. But if you press to exhaustion, you are less likely to climb back on the horse, and if you do get in the saddle, you'll plod from fatigue.
- Create the environment where you work best. If that environment involves a mahogany desk and a fancy leather chair, go for it, but remember that your goal is production, not opulent surroundings. If you look at the desks of the men and women who really crank out quality manuscripts, you'll usually notice a blue-collar aura about the setup. Find out what helps your productivity and incorporate it. For me, it's two or more computer screens, with the ability to cut and paste from one to the other. Even on a single screen, I generally divide the electronic real estate into two. Personally, I don't see why any writer would want to be limited to one screen, flipping back and forth between source material

and manuscript. I also like plenty of light, and more than one observer has remarked that my office looks more like an operating room than a study.

- Get up early. Night owls may disagree, and they may be right, but I believe most people write better in the morning, especially when they have "slept on it" (meaning their work) the night before. There is some scientific basis to the benefits of letting your subconscious work on a problem overnight. Perhaps my preference for morning writing is simply that my brain is too cluttered and clouded at the end of the day to be productive. I usually lay out the next morning's work at night, take note of what I hope to accomplish the next day, and extract myself from the bed as early as I can manage.

STEP 8: GET PAID FOR YOUR WRITING

If your job involves writing in any capacity, you are getting paid for it now. But there are other ways to expand your career as a professional writer, assuming you want to move in that direction and assuming money is important to you. Of course, I don't personally know anyone to whom money is not important, so that may be a moot point.

Let me note that money does more than pay the bills. When you receive money for your writing, it's a psychological boost and a spur to greater professional growth. When someone is paying you for your work, you generally feel an obligation to uphold your end of the transaction with a quality product. Income, then, is a both a reward and a prompt toward greater professional achievement.

A complete guide to writing for money is beyond the scope of this book, but there are many good resources and I have included a couple in the Suggested Readings section.

Let me note at this point that the process of writing for money is reasonably straightforward. In many cases, you develop an idea for a particular type of publication, query that publication, and if successful receive an assignment. You're paid, generally, when the article is accepted or sometimes you are paid when it's published. With books, you prepare a proposal and circulate it (either yourself or through an agent) to publishers, who may pay you an "advance" against future royalties. I have included a sample book proposal in Chapter 11, both as an example of persuasive writing and as a model for you if you want to sell a book.

Emerging digital technologies offer several avenues for payment. An easy but seldom very profitable way is to start a blog and carry ads that Google (or sometimes other companies) automatically and digitally insert into your pages. Another method, which occasionally does produce profit, sometimes substantial, is to publish an electronic book and market it through the Amazon platform or your own website.

The e-book market requires not only that the author in most cases must handle promotion, but also that the author will have an inventory of related products to upsell and cross-market. That may not be as daunting as you might expect, for reasons I discuss in the next entry.

STEP 9: BECOME WIDELY PUBLISHED (OR AT LEAST WELL KNOWN) IN YOUR FIELD, SPECIALTY, OR GENRE

The way professional writers make their money has evolved. Today, many market specialized information in a variety of venues, wearing several professional hats in the process. It's not unusual to see talk show hosts write books or for book writers to branch out into talk shows. Financial consultants give speeches and seminars and almost always blog. Physicians give talks to promote their practice and sometimes their books.

You may be in a profession where writing is part of your job but could also be used as a tool to expand your influence and income. The landscape of full-time employment and freelancing has shifted radically in the past couple of decades as the ability to inexpensively communicate on a large scale has evolved. Today's full-time journalist may be dividing time among a blog, a book, speaking engagements, and talk show appearances. Many of the big names you see on TV are doing just that. Today's full-time athletic trainer may be dividing time and energy among writing a blog, counseling clients, giving talks, and writing Amazon e-books.

Do you see a common denominator in all these equations? I hope so. The ability to write and communicate elegantly is more crucial today than at any time in history and it's imperative to prepare to meet the challenge.

Luckily, you're almost finished with this book, so you'll be well-prepared.

STEP 10: BUILD AN ONLINE PRESENCE

In fact, there's only one thing left to consider: Constructing the mechanism by which you generate exposure and reinforce your brand.

The term "platform" generally is taken to mean your presence on the Internet and other media. When people speak of their platforms, they often refer to their blogs, social media, and Twitter postings. In the mix, more often than not, is a book, either in electronic or in traditional print format, or both.

Remember that the purpose of a platform is synergy, making the pieces work together to create a whole that is bigger than the sum of the parts. A blog, for example, may produce an income and may have a significant revenue from Internet advertising, but it is seldom the end product. In fact, there are no real "end products" in a platform-based writing economy. Each part of the platform nourishes the others. Twitter drives readers to the blog; the blog generates some revenue but serves as a mechanism to promote an online course and a book and speaking engagements. The online book drives people to the course, the blog, and speaking engagements. The speaking tour reciprocates—and an additive chain reaction is set into motion.

Check out Michael Hyatt's blog at MichaelHyatt.com and notice how his alluring content draws readers to many of his products, including the definitive guide to online platforms, not unsurprisingly titled *Platform*, and subtitled *Get Noticed in a Busy World*.

When you read through his material, you'll notice the quality of the writing. Without his engaging tone and diligently researched material, all the synergy in the world would simply fizzle into meaningless entropy.

Good writing is the key to a platform and to professional success. It doesn't really matter whether you call it professional writing, journalism, business writing, public relations, blogging, or what have you. It's about communication that empowers you to get what you want at work, or in life.

It worked for Benjamin Franklin, who recalled in his autobiography that "prose writing has been of great use to me in the course of my life, and was a principal means of my advancement."

It will work for you, too.

Chapter 11

The Ten Techniques in Action: Step-by-Step Demonstrations of the "Write Like a Pro" Techniques in Various Styles of Writing

The purpose of this chapter is to deconstruct some samples and show how they are knitted together using the techniques presented in this book. I'll keep the commentary brief: just enough to indicate the general strategy and flow of the piece. I won't refer to each technique by number because that would quickly become as numbing as watching a bingo game.

I chose the pieces because they were appropriate for a clear demonstration or they were excellently written, or both. Most of what follows is my work, not because it is particularly good but because I know exactly how it is structured, and why.

Included first is a biographical piece that makes extensive use of quotes, anecdotes, and transitions; I have also included the outline to demonstrate how a simple outline can make writing a complex piece into a stress-free exercise of verbal paint-by-the-numbers.

Next is George Orwell's "A Hanging," which is a brilliant piece. It includes the most evocative description I've ever read, plus a perfect "show, don't tell" moment, what I call a "show point."

I have included an opinion piece to demonstrate organization and the use of what I have called "gem quotes." After that, there is a very compelling press release that is exemplary in the way it understands the needs of the reader and the writer.

I follow with a book proposal, for two reasons: First, it's a pretty good example of persuasive writing (that, of course, is what a proposal is) and second, I implore you to consider writing a book, and a proposal is the first step. Even if you self-publish, an outline and a conceptualization of your market is essential. A complete guide to book publishing is beyond the scope of this book, but I offer some sources in the Suggested Readings at the end of this book.

The chapter concludes with an explanation of how sound works and a corporate blog post. I wrote most of the sound explanation, and frankly I'm proud of it. The piece represents my specialty: making complex information understandable. That is a skill useful in any line of writing, and I hope the sample can be used to illustrate the principles in this book, particularly those in Chapter 6. In my case, I believe I changed the approach toward teaching radio news and production nationwide. The book from which the sample comes was published thirty years ago and has been updated and kept in print since that time.

The blog post is from a company that markets technical services but sells them to humans—using marvelously lively and humorous copy.

Eastman Outline

A Sample Outline for a Long and Complex involved Piece — A Biographical Article about George Eastman

This project examined first research at the George Eastman House in Rochester, New York. I had involved access to many of Eastman's original papers and many articles about him.

But how to make sense of it all? It needed a theme—and the theme came to me when I saw a copy of Eastman's suicide note. He was a quirky, methodical man who impressed some of his personality traits on the industry he founded, and in turn changed the very nature of American industry in the late 1800s.

The outline breaks the story into an opening anecdote, the statement of theme, examples of the beginning of his career, the significance of the development of Kodak and its products, a cue that the piece is coming to the end, and a thump at the end.

Take a moment to look through the outline and see how it breaks the story into bite-size pieces. Then read the story and see how it is stitched together. My explanatory notes are in italics.

1. Suicide note—strange nature of man
2. Theme—why strange nature translated into business success

    a. Methodical
    b. Structure was an invention
    c. Examples

3. Transition to background

    Above, I introduced the theme. Then I put it into the context of the era.

4. Show why background—Eastman's and country's—is important to story

    a. Inventions
    b. Industrial Revolution

5. Transition from inventions in general to film

    a. Problem
    b. Solution to wet plate—use funny letter "intimate"

6. Question back to theme—method, "knowledge all empirical"
7. Bring in birth of consumer technology—only a professional could cope (Brady example)
8. Eastman sets mind to find solution

    Now, the focus is on telling interesting stories that keep the reader's attention and illustrate how Eastman accomplished his goals. It's all about showing, not telling.

9. Background—no scientific training, maybe a good thing

    a. Research in kitchen
    b. Driven to overcome poverty . . . foreshadow future   philanthropy

10. His research

    a. More kitchen experiments
    b. Calculating, quality control
    c. Foreshadow mass production idea . . . letter

11. Breakthrough
12. Disaster!

a. What he did—make good

b. Why important—changed nature of business

Here in the outline I decided to spend a lot of the article moving forward chronologically. You don't have to do this, even in a history article, but telling the story chronologically is as good as way as any and better than most. As I advise in the book, sticking to a clear timeline keeps the reader engaged.

13. Once established, where business went . . .

a. Film—invention of substance and use of word

b. Detective camera

c. Marketing to consumer

d. Establishment of name KODAK . . . how tied in to marketing

e. More innovation—

1. Plastic base for film

2. Funny ivory story—invention of celluloid

f. Right up to turn of century, close out discussion with reference to society as in open

You know the part of the flight where you subtly sense that the airplane is headed downward toward landing . . . even though it's a ways away? That's what I want to cue the reader to at this point. I start writing about Eastman's final days.

14. Product story finished—return to Eastman's personality, what it would mean for closing days of company

a. Relationships with women—cold

b. Clune story and quote—cold

15. But he began to change (show movement toward end of story)

a. Employee benefits

b. Music—funny Eastman house story

c. Eastman School of Music

d. Medical care—childhood trauma

e. Travel

16. His declining days—Clune story, show clearly it's near the end

17. Conclusion

a. Didn't invent a lot of stuff, but did invent consumer technology

b. Relate back to historical material, whole country, in beginning and middle of story

c. Moral of story: He invented consumer technology

d. His was a story where "every revolution was once a thought in one person's mind, and when it occurred to others, it was the key to an era"

And now, here is the full story based on the outline you've just read:

George Eastman and the Mirror with a Memory

George Eastman wrote a short note, carefully removed his glasses, placed a towel over his chest, and shot himself through the heart. His final correspondence reflected the calculating, methodical and often quirky character which thrust him to the forefront of American industry.

"To my friends—My work is done. Why wait?"

The purpose of an opening anecdote is to capture attention and draw the reader in. The anecdote has to tell the story behind the story.

As explained in Chapter 8, Step 2, the anecdote should be a story that tells the larger story.

Eastman, who suffered in later life from a degenerative spinal disease, was an independent man who was horrified by the thought of physical infirmity and, especially, by the threat of losing his mental faculties. The coldly methodical nature that compelled him to plan the end of his life—he had previously asked his physician to point out the location of his heart—enabled Eastman to plan and order his massively successful enterprises. In fact, his carefully structured approach to business was something of an invention. The Eastman Dry Plate Company, which would later evolve into the Eastman Kodak Company of Rochester, N.Y., was a pioneer in the field of consumer technology, adopting practices that were to change the complexion of modern business and marketing profoundly.

The preceding paragraphs are the statement of theme . . . telling what the piece will be about. Sometimes it's called the "nut graf" by journalists. It sets the stage for the rest of the article, previewing what is coming.

Among these practices was the introduction of highly technical products to a market of nonscientific users. One hundred years ago, Eastman replaced forever the cumbersome wet-plate system with commercially available transparent roll film, a product easily handled by the consumer and developed by technicians at the factory. 1889 also saw the widespread adoption of the advertising slogan that was to become the blueprint for Kodak's marketing strategy: "You press the button—we do the rest."

Born in rural Upstate New York in 1854, Eastman came of age in an era of technological revolution that dawned in concert with the beginning of the United States' second century. While events of the nation's first century swirled around the political turmoil and philosophies of a largely agricultural population, the second hundred years would begin the U.S. Centennial to the year 1900 saw more than a dozen major inventions, including the telephone (1876), Edison's first version of the phonograph (1877), the electric light (1879), the Linotype (1885), the wireless (1896), along with Eastman's film and roll-holder (1884) and transparent film (1889).

This purpose of the history above is to show how there is a broader significance to the Kodak story.

George Eastman viewed this emerging technological world with characteristic curiosity. Why, Eastman wondered, couldn't the cumbersome process of taking photos be simplified? Eastman had taken up photography in 1878 at 24 after investing a portion of his $1,500-per-annum bank clerk's salary. He soon grew tired of the burdensome paraphernalia. In a rare interview granted toward the end of his career, he recalled that in the 1870s "one did not 'take' a camera; one accompanied an outfit of which the camera was only a part. I bought an outfit and learned that it took not only a strong but a dauntless man to be an outdoor photographer."

It's important to use quotes when possible and when available. This isn't the strongest quote in the world, but it's not bad . . . it gives some insight into Eastman's character.

The heart of the problem was the so-called wet plate, a glass sheet holding the light-sensitive chemical that captured the photographic image. Wet plates had to be coated with a substance called collodion and then sensitized in the field with nitrate of silver. Nitrate of silver was, as Eastman noted, "not a liquid to get intimate with." It was highly corrosive, and had to be carried in a tightly stoppered glass jar. Because the wet plate needed to be initially sensitized and then developed on the spot, a photographer who wanted take on-the-scene pictures obliged to haul his laboratory with him, more often than not on his back. Standard equipment included a tent, as well as devices for mixing chemicals and bathing the plates.

Although the weight of a photographer's setup was a nettling problem, what apparently supremely vexed Eastman's ordered mind was the fact that a photographer often had to improvise his own procedures and formulae. "The knowledge was all empirical," he recalled, "and the chemical reactions in the nitrate of silver bath were complicated; the coated plate would sometimes most unexpectedly and awkwardly fail to function."

It became apparent that until the wet-plate problem was solved, photography would remain an esoteric art. Only a dedicated full-time professional could cope with the vagaries of papers, plates, chemicals of various qualities and composition, and also bear the expense of the equipment.

Furthermore, photography—Greek for "writing with light"—was for all practical purposes limited to the artist's studio. Unless one had a combination wagon-cum-lab on wheels such as Civil War photographer Mathew Brady did—or Eastman's dogged perseverance—outdoor photography was simply too complicated for the amateur.

The "writing with light" detail was included because of my fetish with word origins. But it's interesting, and, I think, keeps the reader's attention.

Eastman realized that the camera, which had been dubbed "the mirror with a memory" in the Brady days, would have to overcome major design obstacles before it could be placed into the hands of the buying public. The wet-plate problem would need to be solved, and the imperfect process that resulted would then have to be modified. Part of the eventual solution involved an unusual sequence of inter-related coincidence and part stemmed from Eastman's insight into the emerging needs of the American consumer—insight gained from his frustration. For Eastman, both avenues began in his mother's kitchen.

I worked the "mirror with a memory" quote because it was colorful—and I thought it would make an excellent, compelling title.

George Eastman had no formal scientific training. In fact, he had been forced to leave school at fourteen because of his family's financial problems. When George was eight, his father died, leaving George, his mother and two older sisters impoverished. Writers who followed Eastman's rise often contend that the conditions of his youth caused Eastman to retain the habits of poverty even when he was a wealthy man, a man who routinely gave away millions but insisted that his torn bedsheets be mended instead of being replaced.

The stories must tell a broader story—and here is a great one, showing something of his background and how poverty affected his worldview.

Eastman secured a job as a three-dollar-per-week messenger for an insurance firm and later found a position with a Rochester bank. His interest in photography did seem rather consuming but his employers thought his hobby innocuous. Eastman was conscientious even if drawn and tired at times.

Notice the transition—"if drawn and tired" in the preceding paragraph, and "haggard appearance" in the next paragraph.

There was good reason for his haggard appearance. Eastman would routinely work throughout the night on kitchen-table chemical experiments to simplify photography. Eastman had read hungrily about new techniques in picture-taking, and was intrigued by reports from Europe about a new type of plate, a "dry" plate to replace the awkward chemical-soaked wet plate. Upon finding a formula for dry-plate manufacture in a photography journal, Eastman began producing and improving his own versions.

He took a European "vacation" during which he studied the emulsions used by dry plate manufacturers. Soon, Eastman, who still kept his day job at the bank, was selling dry plates to photographers.

Were it not for the nature of Eastman's calculating mind, the dry plate might have remained a kitchen-built curiosity for, while Eastman did not invent the dry plate, he did patent a machine to coat plates with a dry emulsion, and soon he invented a broader concept. A letter dated October 13, 1979, to a prospective customer was particularly portentous:

The "calculating mind" reference is to keep the reader on track with the theme—that Eastman's methods set the agenda for an entire generation of industrialists.

. . . I am as yet connected with photography as an amateur only but am making preparations to engage in the manufacture of Gelatine Plates on a large scale and expect my invention, the plate-coaling apparatus, to enable me, if necessary, to put the price down to a point which will prevent miscellaneous competition.

By 1880, Eastman had redesigned his machine. Among other improvements, it could coat a wide variety of plate sizes. In a letter to a New York City firm Eastman noted that as soon as details of manufacturing were "fully systemized, I shall advertise extensively in all the photo-journals and put competent operators on the road to demonstrate the working of the plates."

Note that while it is not a direct transition, the paragraph below echoes the thought of the one above.

Eastman charted his course. Orders for the dry plates accumulated rapidly, and Eastman soon entered into a partnership with a prosperous Rochester businessman, Henry Strong. Strong and Eastman each staked $1,000, and the Eastman Dry Plate Company, now relocated from a kitchen to a downtown factory loft, was fully under way in 1881, only three years after Eastman had taken up photography. Business was brisk and healthy until the spring of 1882. Disaster loomed.

The point of this transition is to build suspense, and it introduces a dramatic element.

The complaints came in rapid-fire. Eastman plates were no good! The chemistry had gone "dead." Eastman checked samples and found that the emulsion on plates stored over the winter had spoiled. He recalled all the plates in use and promised to make good on spoiled plates already purchased. Factory production halted; hundreds of experiments were conducted. Eastman and partner Strong traveled to England in search of an answer.

When it came, that answer was totally unexpected: The fault lay not with Eastman's manufacturing process but with a batch of gelatin that was defective at the time Eastman purchased it from the manufacturer. Now in debt and facing an uncertain future, Eastman vowed to test incoming raw materials and utilize experimental controls to scrutinize the quality of his outgoing product. Business rebounded, in part due to the good will Eastman generated by making good on defective merchandise, a rare practice at the time.

Here again, the reader is brought back to the main point—the agenda that Eastman set.

Even though the business for dry-coated glass plates prospered, Eastman continued to focus on the average man and woman who, even with dry-plate technology, could and would not warm to the bulky equipment of the era and the heavy, fragile glass plates. Eastman knew that replacing the glass plates and simplification of the photographic process were the keys to making his moderately successful business into a vast commercial enterprise.

The easiest transition comes next—"in addition."

In addition, he felt that part of the solution would be some sort of photographic "film," a word which had no connotation with photography at the time. At first, paper seemed to be an ideal vehicle to hold the photosensitive coating. In 1884 Eastman patented a paper-rolling process with which rolls of sensitized paper film could be attached to the backs of existing cameras.

Always look for interesting material to keep the reader's attention. The fact that film had no connotation with photography at the time interested me, so I assumed it would interest the reader.

Paper film, for a time, was the crux of Eastman's revolution in consumer technology. With paper film, many exposures could be taken, and the camera itself could be greatly simplified and miniaturized. Eastman began work on a "detective camera," a popular entry into the growing market of cameras touted as being suitable for secretive use, replacing the wagon-load of equipment needed only a few years before. Eastman's original detective camera never went into full production, though, because it suffered from the same problems as other existing models: It did not produce good-quality photos.

Instead of competing haphazardly for a novelty market, Eastman developed a comprehensive marketing strategy, an ordered approach new to the 1880s. He began by defining his product: a camera that would be more than a detective-camera-type toy but less than a professional rig. It would be a simple-to-operate device that would produce reasonably good-quality photos, and a product inexpensive enough to be purchased by the masses. Eastman then devised a strategy to get the product into the hands of the public. He took the unusual approach of marketing a technological item via mass advertising.

Here is another example of the main theme: Eastman also brought advertising of consumer technology into the mix.

The word Kodak was an initial step in this marketing effort. Eastman wanted a trademark name for his camera that was distinctive. In 1920, Eastman told a reporter for *System Magazine:* "I devised the name myself. . . . The letter 'K' had been a favorite with me—it seems a strong, incisive kind of letter." Eastman tried out many combinations of letters that started and ended with K and finally settled on Kodak, a completely invented word which was an ideal trademark. It was short, incapable of being misspelled so as to destroy its identity, and it fulfilled the basic requirement of trademark law—a standard descriptive word cannot be trademarked.

Another compelling piece of information—a surprise for most readers . . .
Kodak was an invented name designed with memorability in mind.

Simplicity was the second step in Eastman's marketing strategy. Advertisements touted the new camera's ease of use. The Kodak—the word originally applied only to the camera, not the company—was officially introduced on a mass scale in 1888. It was loaded with film at the factory; one hundred shots could be taken and the camera was then returned to the factory where the film was removed and developed and a new roll of film inserted. The Kodak camera sold for $25, including the film, and the processing and new roll of film cost $10.

Eastman would continue to develop marketable innovations in film and cameras. Paper as a base for film still posed a problem. It could not be made completely transparent, and the quality of the resulting photos suffered. In addition, the image on the photosensitive coating had to be physically lifted from the paper base and mounted on a transparent gel before developing. The process was cumbersome and difficult.

Happy coincidence provided the answer. A printer and inventor named John Wesley Hyatt had perfected a substance to replace the ivory in billiard balls (he entered and won a contest sponsored by a manufacturer running short on supplies of ivory). Hyatt's primary ingredient was the substance called collodion, or gun cotton, a chemical that had been utilized in the old wet-plate photo technology. Gun cotton, cotton impregnated with nitric and sulfuric acids, was highly explosive, and there are unconfirmed but intriguing reports of Hyatt's billiard balls exploding in Old West saloons.

Stories, stories, stories . . . the life blood of writing. How could I pass up the
link to exploding billiard balls?

The billiard balls were not the answer to Eastman's film problem; the skin left over from the ersatz ivory-manufacturing process was. Inventor Hyatt had become interested in the commercial possibilities of this skin and, after a series of experiments during which the unschooled Hyatt risked blowing himself to eternity while heating gun cotton in combination with shellac and paper flock, the substance known as celluloid was formed.

Eastman found that celluloid would allow for much more efficient production and developing of film, and this substance would eventually form the base for a practical moving-picture film. Cameras, photographic papers, and the improved flexible film would continue to gain popularity, and Eastman's firm, soon renamed the Eastman Kodak Company, would expand through the remainder of the nineteenth and into the twentieth century. The Rochester manufacturing headquarters would expand to more than 200 buildings covering 2,000 acres, and the firm would become multinational.

This is the beginning of the end of the story. I cue the reader by shifting to some personal, melancholy details of Eastman.

But for all of his understanding of the consumer's psyche, George Eastman did not relate particularly well with others. He was never known to have had a physical relationship with a woman, and his emotional relationships with members of the opposite sex seemed to have been largely limited to weekly luncheons with young wives of associates and employees. It was reported that Eastman subscribed to *Vogue* magazine in an effort to establish a common ground for communication with these young companions.

He was generally quite cool in his relationships with other people. Henry Clune, who worked as a reporter for a Rochester newspaper, 98 at the time he was interviewed for this article, remembers Eastman as polite but distant. Asked for a description of Eastman, Clune read from a book he had published in 1983:

The Clune interview was a wonderful opportunity and, in my opinion, considerably elevated the story. Here was the man who was possibly the last living link to Eastman.

George Eastman was a man of medium stature, sedentary in appearance and habit, with a paunch that protruded slightly under the white waistcoat he often wore. He had a cold eye behind steel-rimmed spectacles, a tight mouth, and a personality that encouraged human intercourse with something less than the quick response of iron filings to the attraction of a magnet. He was a bachelor, who perhaps needed a cutie in his life and probably never had one. He once said he never laughed until he was forty.

Eastman devoted himself single-mindedly to control of the nation's photographic industry and, that accomplished, this seemingly cold-blooded magnate began to change. The new, more human direction was to transform many aspects of Kodak, the city of Rochester, and American industry in general.

To begin with, he introduced a comprehensive series of employee benefits. Eastman initiated a savings program, sickness and accident benefits, and in 1912 introduced the concept of a wage dividend, a move that gave employees a direct stake in the profitability of the company for the first time. Music became rather an obsession with Eastman. Although he was reputed to be practically tone-deaf, Eastman hired an organist to play every morning during breakfast. The organ, organist, and Eastman were housed in an opulent mansion that became the site of many a musical event. Eastman, truly the perfectionist, had the mansion cut in half, moved on its foundations, and partially rebuilt so that the center chamber could have better acoustics.

A fascinating detail.
And a transition using the word "music."

Eastman's love of music would later motivate the establishment of the Eastman School of Music, a noted Rochester conservatory, and the construction of a grand concert hall called the Eastman Theater. His largess extended to the University of Rochester and to the Massachusetts Institute of Technology. Eastman once gave two-and-a-half million dollars to MIT as an anonymous gift and then made other substantial contributions under his own name when solicited by MIT fund-raisers.

Perhaps because of a childhood experience watching his mother having a tooth pulled at the kitchen table, Eastman directed much of his philanthropy to the study and practice of dentistry. He built a massive dental clinic in Rochester and eventually funded dental dispensaries in London, Paris, Rome, Brussels, and Stockholm.

For all of his generosity, it seemed that Eastman lived out his life a rather sad and lonely man. Travels occupied much of his time; he would virtually conscript people to travel with him. On one occasion, Eastman summoned the wife of his staff organist to travel overseas to meet him so that he would have company on the return trip.

Newspaperman Clune recalls a macabre meeting with Eastman that took place within months of Eastman's death.

Now the plane is clearly in its descent. The wheels are coming down. But the quotes keep the piece lively.

I always had trouble getting past his Amazon housekeeper.

When I showed up for an interview set up by Mr. Gannett [the newspaper's publisher] she wouldn't let me in—said that Mr. Eastman was sick. Finally, she let me in but said I could only stay 10 minutes.

Eastman was lying down, fully dressed. I did the interview—I don't remember what it was about—and prepared to leave. As I walked away, Eastman asked me if I wanted to see his guns, I said, "yes sir," as everyone did say to Eastman, even though I didn't care about guns at all. Eastman took me to a room filled with fishing rods and guns and showed me these elephant guns—and I remember his hands shook so badly that he dropped parts of the guns on the floor.

Clune again edged toward the door but Eastman seemed anxious to prolong the visit. "I started to go and he said, 'Let's look at some pictures.' He showed me some films of employees' children playing on the lawn, and said they were a damn sight more graceful than some of the dancers at his theater. I left after that, but I think he wanted me to stay. He was a lonely old man."

This is the first trial ending. As in music, there is a process of wrapping up—endings that don't quite end—and then closing with a thump. Here's the thump—a summary that wraps the story back to the beginning. The echo effect makes it seem like a cohesive whole.

George Eastman did not invent consumer technology full-blown, in one grand stroke, any more than Thomas Edison could be credited with inventing the process of inventing. Eastman, like Edison, and like the other innovators who moved America into the new century, often borrowed ideas from others and synthesized those ideas into new ways of doing things.

George Eastman certainly did not invent photography, or dry plates, or the portable camera. If he can be credited with discrete discoveries, those discoveries are ones of process. He refined the process of putting a technological product directly into the hands of the public, complete with simplified operating instructions. Part of this process involved mass production at low per-unit cost. The genius of his plan was an interrelated flow of product from factory floor to purchaser.

Along the way, he bolstered some industrial practices that proved a model for other industries. In-house industrial research and development constituted a process for which Eastman could rightly claim to be a pioneer. Fair treatment and profit sharing for employees proved successful for Eastman. While his motives may not have been entirely altruistic, the bottom line reinforced the wisdom of his personnel practices. Such principles seem obvious or even simplistic today, but in the nineteenth century they were unusual.

Sometimes it doesn't hurt to show how you have made your points. It's like a victory lap.

Ideas and discoveries in the era of Eastman meshed, interacted, and synthesized, virtually assuming a life of their own. The growing availability of scientific papers and journals helped many innovators, including Eastman, to integrate the ideas of others. Increased opportunities for travel and the figurative shrinking of the scientific and business worlds allowed ideas to multiply.

Indeed, as Emerson noted, "Every revolution was first a thought in one man's mind, and when the same thought occurs to another man, it is the key to that era."[1]

Not the best quote, but it serves the purpose . . . an interesting statement that satisfies and makes the piece complete.

An Example of a Piece Using Vivid Description and Evocative Action

"A Hanging"

By George Orwell (Eric Arthur Blair)

Here is a terrific example of description that brings prose to life. Moreover, it includes a brilliant example of a story that tells a story.

It was in Burma, a sodden morning of the rains. A sickly light, like yellow tinfoil, was slanting over the high walls into the jail yard. We were waiting outside the condemned cells, a row of sheds fronted with double bars, like small animal cages. Each cell measured about ten feet by ten and was quite bare within except for a plank bed and a pot of drinking water. In some of them brown silent men were squatting at the inner bars, with their blankets draped round them. These were the condemned men, due to be hanged within the next week or two.

Yellow tinfoil . . . an unusual but extraordinarily vivid comparison.

One prisoner had been brought out of his cell. He was a Hindu, a puny wisp of a man, with a shaven head and vague liquid eyes. He had a thick, sprouting moustache, absurdly too big for his body, rather like the moustache of a comic man on the films. Six tall Indian warders were guarding him and getting him ready for the gallows. Two of them stood by with rifles and fixed bayonets, while the others handcuffed him, passed a chain through his handcuffs and fixed it to their belts, and lashed his arms tight to his sides. They crowded very close about him, with their hands always on him in a careful, caressing grip, as though all the while feeling him to make sure he was there. It was like men handling a fish which is still alive and may jump back into the water. But he stood quite unresisting, yielding his arms limply to the ropes, as though he hardly noticed what was happening.

Note how the precise and imaginative description makes the scene come alive.

Eight o'clock struck and a bugle call, desolately thin in the wet air, floated from the distant barracks. The superintendent of the jail, who was standing apart from the rest of us, moodily prodding the gravel with his stick, raised his head at the sound. He was an army doctor, with a grey toothbrush moustache and a gruff voice. "For God's sake hurry up, Francis," he said irritably. "The man ought to have been dead by this time. Aren't you ready yet?"

Sometimes adverbs work, as in the preceding paragraph. The action illuminates the scene.

Francis, the head jailer, a fat Dravidian in a white drill suit and gold spectacles, waved his black hand. "Yes sir, yes sir," he bubbled. "All iss satisfactorily prepared. The hangman iss waiting. We shall proceed."

"Well, quick march, then. The prisoners can't get their breakfast till this job's over."

It's always risky to quote in dialect, as Orwell does here with "iss" but in this piece, an essay, it works.

We set out for the gallows. Two warders marched on either side of the prisoner, with their rifles at the slope; two others marched close against him, gripping him by arm and shoulder, as though at once pushing and supporting him. The rest of us, magistrates and the like, followed behind. Suddenly, when we had gone ten yards, the procession stopped short without any order or warning. A dreadful thing had happened, a dog, come goodness knows whence, had appeared in the yard. It came bounding among us with a loud volley of barks, and leapt round us wagging its whole body, wild with glee at finding so many human beings together. It was a large woolly dog, half Airedale, half pariah. For a moment it pranced round us, and then, before anyone could stop it, it had made a dash for the prisoner, and jumping up tried to lick his face. Everyone stood aghast, too taken aback even to grab at the dog.

As explained in the book, highlighting ironies adds power to the piece. Here, Orwell is contrasting the macabre execution scenario with a dog playing on the grounds . . . the point being that the dog is normal, but what's happening is decidedly not.

"Who let that bloody brute in here?" said the superintendent angrily. "Catch it, someone!"

A warder, detached from the escort, charged clumsily after the dog, but it danced and gambolled just out of his reach, taking everything as part of the game. A young Eurasian jailer picked up a handful of gravel and tried to stone the dog away, but it dodged the stones and came after us again. Its yaps echoed from the jail walls. The prisoner, in the grasp of the two warders, looked on incuriously, as though this was another formality of the hanging. It was several minutes before someone managed to catch the dog. Then we put my handkerchief through its collar and moved off once more, with the dog still straining and whimpering.

It was about forty yards to the gallows. I watched the bare brown back of the prisoner marching in front of me. He walked clumsily with his bound arms, but quite steadily, with that bobbing gait of the Indian who never straightens his knees. At each step his muscles slid neatly into place, the lock of hair on his scalp danced up and down, his feet printed themselves on the wet gravel. And once, in spite of the men who gripped him by each shoulder, he stepped slightly aside to avoid a puddle on the path.

In the next paragraph comes the main point . . . Orwell's horror at seeing a living man moments away from death. He points this out by showing and not telling—through vivid description and the "show point" where the man, in his native humanness, avoids a puddle, despite the fact he will die in moments.

It is curious, but till that moment I had never realized what it means to destroy a healthy, conscious man. When I saw the prisoner step aside to avoid the puddle, I saw the mystery, the unspeakable wrongness, of cutting a life short when it is in full tide. This man was not dying, he was alive just as we were alive. All the organs of his body were working, bowels digesting food, skin renewing itself, nails growing, tissues forming, all toiling away in solemn foolery. His nails would still be growing when he stood on the drop, when he was falling through the air with a tenth of a second to live. His eyes saw the yellow gravel and the grey walls, and his brain still remembered, foresaw, reasoned, reasoned even about puddles. He and we were a party of men walking together, seeing, hearing, feeling, understanding the same world; and in two minutes, with a sudden snap, one of us would be gone, one mind less, one world less.

The gallows stood in a small yard, separate from the main grounds of the prison, and overgrown with tall prickly weeds. It was a brick erection like three sides of a shed, with planking on top, and above that two beams and a crossbar with the rope dangling. The hangman, a grey-haired convict in the white uniform of the prison, was waiting beside his machine. He greeted us with a servile crouch as we entered. At a word from Francis the two warders, gripping the prisoner more closely than ever, half led, half pushed him to the gallows and helped him clumsily up the ladder. Then the hangman climbed up and fixed the rope round the prisoner's neck.

Notice how all the venues are described—including the "rough circle" around the gallows.

We stood waiting, five yards away. The warders had formed in a rough circle round the gallows. And then, when the noose was fixed, the prisoner began crying out on his god. It was a high, reiterated cry of "Ram! Ram! Ram! Ram!," not urgent and fearful like a prayer or a cry for help, but steady, rhythmical, almost like the tolling of a bell. The dog answered the sound with a whine. The hangman, still standing on the gallows, produced a small cotton bag like a flour bag and drew it down over the prisoner's face. But the sound, muffled by the cloth, still persisted, over and over again: "Ram! Ram! Ram! Ram! Ram!"

The hangman climbed down and stood ready, holding the lever. Minutes seemed to pass. The steady, muffled crying from the prisoner went on and on, "Ram! Ram! Ram!" never faltering for an instant. The superintendent, his head on his chest, was slowly poking the ground with his stick; perhaps he was counting the cries, allowing the prisoner a fixed number, fifty, perhaps, or a hundred. Everyone had changed color. The Indians had gone grey like bad coffee, and one or two of the bayonets were wavering. We looked at the lashed, hooded man on the drop, and listened to his cries, each cry another second of life; the same thought was in all our minds: oh, kill him quickly, get it over, stop that abominable noise!

Grey like bad coffee . . . bayonets were wavering. Clear, vivid description.

Suddenly the superintendent made up his mind. Throwing up his head he made a swift motion with his stick. "Chalo!" he shouted almost fiercely.

There was a clanking noise, and then dead silence. The prisoner had vanished, and the rope was twisting on itself. I let go of the dog, and it galloped immediately to the back of the gallows; but when it got there it stopped short, barked, and then retreated into a corner of the yard, where it stood among the weeds, looking timorously out at us. We went round the gallows to inspect the prisoner's body. He was dangling with his toes pointed straight downwards, very slowly revolving, as dead as a stone.

The superintendent reached out with his stick and poked the bare body; it oscillated, slightly. "He's all right," said the superintendent. He backed out from under the gallows, and blew out a deep breath. The moody look had gone out of his face quite suddenly. He glanced at his wrist-watch. "Eight minutes past eight. Well, that's all for this morning, thank God."

The warders unfixed bayonets and marched away. The dog, sobered and conscious of having misbehaved itself, slipped after them. We walked out of the gallows yard, past the condemned cells with their waiting prisoners, into the big central yard of the prison. The convicts, under the command of warders armed with lathis, were already receiving their breakfast. They squatted in long rows, each man holding a tin pannikin, while two warders with buckets marched round ladling out rice; it seemed quite a homely, jolly scene, after the hanging. An enormous relief had come upon us now that the job was done. One felt an impulse to sing, to break into a run, to snigger. All at once everyone began chattering gaily.

Again, the actions (ladling) and the substances (tin) are included to keep the mental scene playing.

The Eurasian boy walking beside me nodded towards the way we had come, with a knowing smile: "Do you know, sir, our friend (he meant the dead man), when he heard his appeal had been dismissed, he pissed on the floor of his cell. From fright. Kindly take one of my cigarettes, sir. Do you not admire my new silver case, sir? From the boxwallah, two rupees eight annas. Classy European style."

Several people laughed, at what, nobody seemed certain.

Francis was walking by the superintendent, talking garrulously. "Well, sir, all hass passed off with the utmost satisfactoriness. It wass all finished, flick! like that. It iss not always so, oah, no! I have known cases where the doctor wass obliged to go beneath the gallows and pull the prisoner's legs to ensure decease. Most disagreeable!"

"Wriggling about, eh? That's bad," said the superintendent.

"Ach, sir, it iss worse when they become refractory! One man, I recall, clung to the bars of hiss cage when we went to take him out. You will scarcely credit, sir, that it took six warders to dislodge him, three pulling at each leg. We reasoned with him. 'My dear fellow,' we said, 'think of all the pain and trouble you are causing to us!' But no, he would not listen! Ach, he wass very troublesome!"

I found that I was laughing quite loudly. Everyone was laughing. Even the superintendent grinned in a tolerant way. "You'd better all come out and have a drink," he said quite genially. "I've got a bottle of whisky in the car. We could do with it."

We went through the big double gates of the prison, into the road. "Pulling at his legs!" exclaimed a Burmese magistrate suddenly, and burst into a loud chuckling. We all began laughing again. At that moment Francis's anecdote seemed extraordinarily funny. We all had a drink together, native and European alike, quite amicably. The dead man was a hundred yards away.[2]

An Example of Using Techniques of Persuasion in an Opinion Piece

Lessons from Lyin' Brian: It's Time to Reinvent TV News

By Carl Hausman

News events are obvious prompts for opinion pieces. In this case, the point was not condemnation of Brian Williams for his deceptive reporting, but rather a call for changing what I view as a hopelessly old-fashioned way of delivering the news.

Let me make it clear I'm not defending Brian Williams. I'm just pointing out that his downfall is as much our fault as his.

The opening line is meant to hook attention . . . why, the reader asks, (I hope) is Williams's problem the reader's fault?

Williams essentially got in lockstep with the program imposed by NBC, which relentlessly trumpeted the notion that he was a larger-than-life figure who had been there and done that, was omnipotent and omnipresent, and thus somehow infused credibility into the words he read from a TelePrompTer.

There's no question that pneumatically inflating your persona by lying about your derring-do on the job is an automatic disqualification for a network anchorman, regardless of the intensity of the pressure to live up to the image confected by your bosses' promotion machine.

But think about the underlying issue and our tacit complicity: When we sit down to watch today's incarnation of TV news, aren't we engaged in a certain suspension of disbelief right from the moment we're galvanized by the sweeping theme music? Do we really believe that graying hair and a resonant voice impart credibility? Are we actually buying the conceit that the video snippet harvested by inserting and quickly extracting the combination anchor/star into a war zone somehow creates authenticity?

Here I attempt to invoke consistency by getting the reader to agree with my first, most modest contention. By doing it this way, instead of issuing a blanket proclamation, I hope to get more readers in the tent—gradually.

Suspension of disbelief, of course, is what show business is all about. And the current model for TV news evolved from a time when the medium had to adopt entertainment values in order to seamlessly co-exist with the rest of the broadcast day.

The golden-throated "announcer" descended from masters of ceremonies on stage and in early radio.

Some history here. I am attempting to show how the practices I criticize were reasonable at one time. In essence, I am acknowledging conflicting arguments.

TV-news formats were created to quantify the amount and nature of captivating video to match the visual appeal of entertainment programming. The same formats mandated selection of stories featuring danger and conflict because they aped the engrossing and familiar structure of most drama.

Highly sophisticated and rigorously researched formats resulted in virtually identical pairings of bantering middle-aged men and young blonds stamped out as anchor pairs in city after city. Anchors were tested for likeability by playing tapes of their performance to audiences who were instructed to twist dials to indicate if the anchors made them feel warm and fuzzy.

Still, though, we were given a pretty good product. We didn't get a nightly civics lesson, but we did get some important news packaged by talented people who generally did their best to balance the integrity of the product with the unflinching demand to attract the eyeballs of a mass, undifferentiated audience.

But that mass audience is disappearing. The audience is fragmenting among logarithmically multiplying destinations for those eyeballs.

Network television ratings have officially fallen off the cliff, and in response networks have ratcheted up by doing more of what worked in the past: trying to sell the cult of celebrity.

Today, though, the best guess among media prognosticators is that the strategy for success is to concede that you will reach a smaller audience but seek a devoted and profitable demographic and offer a leaner, more efficient product.

Now I'm getting to my immodest proposal. I have already set the stage by contending that things are changing anyway—toward narrow audiences— so maybe we should take advantage of that trend.

With that assumption in mind, I have an immodest proposal: Let's regroup and reinvent the product. Instead of investing extravagant amounts of cash into promoting the packaged, promoted, and scientifically certified warm-and-fuzzy anchor—in hopes of saving an enterprise that's on life-support anyway—why not hire an extra dozen competent if less-fuzzy reporters?

Now, example after example builds the case.

Instead of the D-Day scale mobilization necessary to parachute the star into the hot spot de jour, why not plow the money back into re-establishing the overseas bureaus that have been eliminated in corporate cost-cutting massacres?

If we absolutely insist on an attractive person mouthing the news, why not follow the lead of many British broadcasters and hire talented but essentially interchangeable personnel we unabashedly identify as news readers or news presenters—shifting the focus to the product instead of the personality?

I realize that everyone who fancies themselves a news aficionado advocates at least some of the above, but now is the time such an approach could actually work. It may have to.

Wouldn't a smaller, but still substantial, audience seek out the type of product that network news organizations, with their vast non-star talent pool and distinguished institutional memory, can provide?

Posing direct questions recaptures reader attention.

After all, news audiences can be catnip to advertisers. Although they tend to skew older than the coveted youthful demographics, news viewers tend to be attentive and thus attractive targets for advertisers. (News audiences are usually watching the program rather than having it on as background chatter.) Also, news audiences are typically more affluent than viewers for other types of programming.

What do we have to lose given the inevitable fragmentation of mass audiences? Would it be such a risk for networks to exploit the true value of TV news—a window on the world that brings us reality and context—rather than to package the news as a constellation of mass entertainment revolving around a few evening stars?

A trial close. What do we have to lose? I hope you are now nodding in agreement.

The deal would have to work both ways, of course. We, as a collective audience, would have to give up the comfort of personality-driven journalism and the familiar warmth of news presented in a show-business frame.

It won't be easy, because we like the mythology that Brian Williams tried too hard to create. Former Librarian of Congress Daniel Boorstin nailed it all the way back in 1962 in a prescient book titled *The Image: A Guide to Pseudo-Events in America.*

Closing with a quote works well. As explained in Chapter 9, Step 9, there's no need to reinvent the wheel. Boorstin said it better that I can. . . .

We hardly dare face our bewilderment about the gap between reality and the ginned-up media experience, he argued, "because our ambiguous experience is so pleasantly iridescent, and the solace of belief in contrived reality is so thoroughly real. We have become eager accessories to the great hoaxes of the age. These are the hoaxes we play on ourselves."[3]

Press Release

An Example of a Press Release That Engages the Reader's Attention

The goal of a press release is to garner favorable publicity. But no media outlet will use your press release if it isn't interesting. Here's an excellent example of an intriguing release that makes it clear the author knew what was in it for the reader and the author.

New Ecommerce Data: Ecommerce Customer Loyalty Is Rare
June 3, 2015 | Janessa Lantz
*May 29, 2015 (Philadelphia, Pa.)—RJMetrics 2015 Ecommerce Buyer
Behavior Benchmark shows lack of customer attachment; 68% of cus-
tomers never purchase a second time.*

New data released today by RJMetrics, a complete analytics platform
for ecommerce, SaaS, and mobile businesses, digs into the behavior of
the ecommerce customer. The biggest finding: while many retailers
tout the benefits of customer retention, most customers never purchase a second time. Only 32% of customers purchase again within a
year of their first purchase.

This is the classic inverted pyramid formula.

These results paint a picture of a very cutthroat industry, where retailers
are constantly in the process of getting in front of new customers, and then
dealing with them on a very transactional basis. This is contrary to the
prevailing narrative within the industry, which tends to emphasize customer relationships and building strong brand advocates. In reality, most
ecommerce companies struggle to get their customers back in the door.

*OK ... companies are doing things wrong. How do they do things right?
The answer comes in the next paragraph.*

But the report surfaced another finding: in spite of these challenges, the
most successful ecommerce companies are building longer-term customer
relationships. Top quartile companies (ranked by growth rate) have customer lifetime values that are 79% higher than their less successful peers.

The report offers two suggestions on how companies can replicate
the success of top performers:

- **First, focus retention efforts on high-value customers**. The report
  found that the top 1% of customers are 18x more valuable than the average customer. Remarketing to these customers to get them back in the
  door has the potential to yield phenomenal ROI.
- **Second, use data to predict who these high-value customers will be**.
  Data from the report shows that top quartile customers spend nearly
  6x more than average customers in their first 30 days. This, combined
  with internal data on things like product categories purchased, acqui-
  sition source, or days between order, can help retailers build simple
  prediction models to identify who has the potential to become a loyal
  customer.

*So ... what's in it for the reader? Advice on running a tech business. What's
in it for the writer? The piece is from a company that advises tech business.*

"While retailers love talking about building brands that customers love, there are very few companies doing that successfully," said RJMetrics CEO, Robert J. Moore. "If you're one of the few retailers who has figured out how to keep your customers coming back you're on the path to something very big."

Interesting quote. Quotes are always a plus in almost any sort of writing.

All this data, and more, can be found in the 2015 Ecommerce Buyer Behavior Benchmark.

About RJMetrics

RJMetrics is the analytics platform of choice for many of the fastest-growing online businesses in the world, including NoMoreRack, Hootsuite, Walker & Company Brands, and more. It provides business users with an easy-to-use, cloud-based solution to drive growth through smarter decision-making. For more information on RJMetrics, visit their website.

Media inquiries:
Janessa Lantz
press@rjmetrics.com

An Example of a Book Proposal — Presented Both as an Example of Persuasive Writing and a Sample You Can Use for Your Own Book Proposal

Here's an example of a persuasive business-plan type of document. I say it's persuasive because I have proof. (I sold the book.) Here's a case where I melded the needs of the writer (selling the book to a publisher) and the needs of the reader (publishers need books they can publish). Note that the proposal is more than a decade old and some of the scenarios referred to here may have changed over the years.

Remember, as we've done throughout this section, my comments are in italics.

LIES WE LIVE BY

By Carl Hausman

Proposal

I'm going to lie to you. And you won't be able to catch me because everything I say will be true. But it's still going to be a lie.

It's critical to grab readers' attention at the outset. People in all businesses receive solicitations all the time. Anything (within reason) you can do to stand out increases your chances.

Watch me as I use facts and figures to sell you on a very expensive investment—an education at a private university.

> "University X is highly selective, accepting only 33 percent of applicants. The average SAT score is 1095. As a result of the high caliber of our student body, we were named one of the outstanding colleges in the East by a well-known national magazine!"

Judging from this information, University X looks like a fine place to drop about $15,000 a year on tuition. It is, after all, exclusive. It admits only one in three applicants. (Obviously, not everybody can be a University X student!) The SAT score is well above the national average—showing, it seems, that this is a competitive college where the standards are high. Correct?

The setup is above. Posing a question is a good way to keep readers' attention. Now comes the answer. . . .

Not really. I've just lied to you, not by what I've said, but by what I've left out. Here's the rest of the story:

- At University X, we don't like it known that we accept most of the people who apply, so we massage the numbers. For starters, we recently began handing out pre-addressed postcards at high schools; students were instructed to fill in their names and mail the postcard for more information. We count that postcard as an "application." Because few of these students go to the next step—filling out a real application—we cut our "acceptance" rate significantly. We also started encouraging applications from students who had virtually no chance of acceptance.
- To cement our reputation as a "selective" college we counted people who were rejected by one program in the university but accepted by another program as rejects. We then further whittled that figure by putting about 500 students on a "waiting list." We accepted most of them later, but still counted them as rejected applicants.
- What about that high "average" SAT? Well, our actual SAT is about 200 points lower. But in order to boost the average we simply did not count people who don't do well on the test, such as international students and students in remedial programs. We also exclude the football team (sturdy folks but not a genius among them) by admitting them when

they show up for training in August instead of the September class. Our "average" SAT score is, of course, computed only on the September class.

As a result of our numbers massage, University X may find itself moving up five or ten slots in the "Best College" rankings of respected publications that may not comprehensively fact-check the data.

The example is hypothetical but the widespread numberfudging is real. When the *Wall Street Journal* compared the figures given in guidebooks with statistics provided to credit rating agencies such as Moody's, the *Journal* found that in virtually every case the guidebook figures were much more favorable to the college, having been massaged with the techniques above and some others even more imaginative. (We name names and blow the whistle in Chapter 7.) It's probably a violation of federal securities law to lie to Moody's, but it's legal to lie to the guidebooks—so in almost every case the "real," uncooked figures were given to Moody's.

Example, example, example. Always provide them, and make them as interesting as possible.

Telling lies is not unique to education, although it is a particularly expensive type of misrepresentation—as well as a galling example of lies told by people who would surely regard themselves as living on a higher moral plane than used car salesmen or fast-talking telemarketers. But very few used cars or aluminum siding jobs cost what a college education does.

* * *

The example above shows one way to lie with the truth. There are many others. But the phony figures provided by some colleges and universities are excellent examples of the modern lie in this media-driven age: a half-truth, a mix of fact and factoid that often makes its point as much by what's left but as by what's put in.

Now, the sales pitch begins. Here's how the book will meet the stated problems . . .

Lies We Live By will show how such lies are crafted, how they sometimes are repeated uncritically and take on a life of their own, and how the lie has become something of an American art form. In the first book-part, we'll provide a crash course in how to lie with words, numbers, and images.

In Part II, we scrutinize various industries that have shown themselves to be less than pristine in their handling of the truth. Part III is a call to action—a prescription for accurate analysis, for detecting the lies we live by, and becoming a resistance fighter for the whole truth.

As stated in the book, it's important to establish credentials. The important thing, though, is to stress credentials that relate to the needs of the reader. Note how I stress my interest in promotion. Publishers often worry that they will sign an author who will be reluctant to promote the work with media appearances.

Remember, this was a few years ago. If I were writing this proposal today, I would also include information about my social media platforms.

About the Author

Carl Hausman is a journalist and educator who has written two books about media ethics, edited a magazine about ethics in international affairs, and has testified about communications ethics before Congress. Hausman is a professor of journalism at Rowan University in Glassboro, New Jersey, and an adjunct professor of journalism at New York University, where he developed and teaches a workshop in explanatory journalism.

He holds a Ph.D. in journalism and media from the Union Graduate School and completed a post-doctoral fellowship at New York University, where he was awarded the Mellon Fellowship in the Humanities.

The author of a total of 19 books (most of them dealing with media) and about 500 published articles, Hausman specializes in making complex subjects simple and interesting. His writing has been called "excellent" by the *New York Times* and "lively and accessible" by *Booklist*. Hausman is a former television talk show host who is comfortable with the book—promotion process and has appeared as a guest on many radio and television talk shows (including the *Morton Downey Jr. Show*).

When not coyly writing his bio in the third person, Hausman frequently lectures on mass media issues and is a subscriber to George Bernard Shaw's maxim: "If you want to tell the public the truths you'd better make them laugh or they'll kill you."

Here's my strategy. I give the overview first, and then the details. The table of contents first, then the outline.

I begin the process with the heading "About the Book".

About the Book

Lies We Live By deals with a serious subject, but relating to the point mentioned above, its approach will be lively. The last thing the world needs, in my view, is another overheated, self-important jeremiad. But at the same time, *Lies We Live By* will be journalistic and to-the-point. We'll name names and shine a flashlight in the eyes of some people and industries that truly deserve the glare. What follows is a proposed table of contents and a brief chapter-by-chapter outline of the book.

Contents

Part 1: The Truth About Lies

1. Lies: The Truth, the Half-Truth, and Nothing Like the Truth
2. How to Lie with Words
3. How to Lie with Numbers
4. How to Lie with Images

Part 2: Would They Lie? Tricks and Techniques of 10 Industries

5. Politics
6. Airlines
7. Education
8. Financial Institutions
9. The Mass Media
10. Lawyers
11. Tobacco Companies
12. The Auto Industry
13. Retail
14. Public Relations
15. Advertising

Part 3: Fighting Back

16. Keeping Distortion in Proportion
17. Resources: Books, People, and Organizations

While I call what follows the "outline," it's really a sales piece as much as an indication of the content.

Outline

Part 1: The Truth About Lies

Chapter 1: Lies: The Truth, the Half-Truth, and Nothing Like the Truth

This introductory chapter provides a brief overview of the industry of lying in America, comparing the "big" lie, which is a blatant falsehood, and the "little lie," which involves a half-truth leading to a conclusion in which there's usually no truth. Chapter 1 includes a brief anecdotal history of lying, featuring politicians, tobacco companies, and other stalwarts, and demonstrates how the lie has today often become a standard technique of doing business.

Chapter 2: How to Lie with Words

Many arguments sound reasonable until we dissect them. For example, a political ad I heard recently touted a new proposal to change the legal system in a way that would (surprise!) benefit trial lawyers. The ad concluded with the announcer intoning, "Recent polls show 84 percent of Americans want a better legal system." Aside from the unexplained linkage between the poll data and the proposal, listeners were given no clue as to how the evidence was concocted. What was the question asked in the poll? Is it any surprise that when asked, "Do you want the legal system to be better or worse?" most people said "better"? (And where did the 14 percent come from who want the system to be worse? Were they the criminals?) In Chapter 2 we'll categorize various kinds of word-lies, from leaps of logic to weasel words (hollow words and phrases that have no meaning), and provide some intriguing examples and anecdotes.

Remember, if you are selling writing, you have to keep the writing lively. That's why I use anecdotes in the outline.

Chapter 3: How to Lie with Numbers

An ad for a chiropractor caught my attention recently. It noted that people injured on the job who seek care from a chiropractor recover 30 percent more quickly than those who are injured and seek care from an M.D. And the chiropractor's patients spend 40 percent less money for treatment. Persuasive! But this is an example of a statistical fallacy called ignoring the exposure base, meaning that the sample from which the original data was drawn is skewed. In this case, it's the assumption that people injured on the job who visit a chiropractor or an M.D. have equivalent injuries. But are they comparable? Would, for example, the fellow who had his legs torn off in a threshing machine drag himself on bloody stumps for a chiropractic adjustment? Probably not . . . he'd more than likely go to an M.D. in the emergency room for a long and expensive recovery. Chapter 3 details the many ways a liar can slant statistics, providing examples and anecdotes.

Chapter 4: How to Lie with Images

Which stock would you buy . . . stock the company whose earnings are represented by Fig. 11.1 or Fig. 11.2?

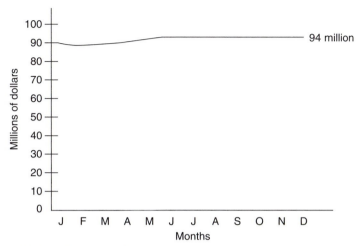

Figure 11.1 An honest graph. The left axis starts at zero, and the increase in earnings is depicted in true proportion. (Figure created by author.)

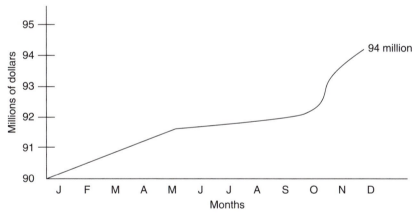

Figure 11.2 A dishonest graph. Sometimes this is called a "Gee Whiz" graph. The increase in earnings is the same as in 11.1, but by tinkering with the axis—chopping off the bottom—I can give the impression of the earnings shooting skyward. (Figure created by author.)

The earnings record shown in 11.2 seems much more impressive. But if you look closely at the graph, you'll see that the earnings are *the same*. I've tinkered with the values of the graph and truncated the bottom. In a shorthand world with time-starved readers, the visual is often the quickest way to communicate and the most effective way to deceive. Chapter 4 shows all the tricks and techniques, and catches some of the perpetrators in the act.

Part 2: Would They Lie? Tricks and Techniques of 10 Industries

Chapter 5: Politics

Chapter 5 begins the book-part that dissects the techniques of telling lies. In politics, we deal with not only with explicit lies, but lies that have become embedded in our framework of ideas. This chapter shows how political candidates use research to uncover the emotional hot buttons that will respond to lies and propaganda. We'll dissect some intentionally misleading ads, such as the Willie Horton ad, which used a juxtaposition of visuals and audio to create a completely false impression. Chapter 5 shows how politicians often frame their statements in ways that dissemble or create false impressions. (One of my favorite examples is a politician who wanted to be seen as tough on crime and ran a spot claiming, "I believe in mandatory life in prison for murderers, and my opponent doesn't." True! His opponent was running on a capital-punishment platform.)

Chapter 6: Airlines

This industry is driven by competition, not only in pricing but in who can out-lie whom in their advertising. Among other issues, we'll examine a recent government investigation showing that many of the "bargain" fares carried so many restrictions that it was virtually impossible to get them. (One ad touted a fare that expired the day before the ad ran.) We'll name names, show examples, and try some experiments to see if we can get those "bargain" fares.

Chapter 7: Education

The same ivory-tower dwellers who castigate the corporate world for its coarseness and slavish obedience to the bottom line tell some of the more egregious lies known in American marketing. The massage of admission statistics detailed in the opening of this proposal would likely land someone in jail if it were done for a stock offering. But that is little consolation to parents and students who fork over astronomical amounts of money and base decisions with life-long impact on falsified figures and empty, illogical words. We'll expose the whole mechanism of deceit in Chapter 7.

Chapter 8: Financial Institutions

Have you ever read the fine print on your credit card statements? They are often masterpieces of misstatement. The rate "promised" will often not be the rate you get. Your pre-"approval" may turn out to be a pre-"approval" that means it was approved that somebody mail you the application form—and you'll be rejected for the promised rate (for which you thought you were pre-approved) and lumped into a category where the rates and fees are higher.

Chapter 9: The Mass Media

A reporter with an ax to grind can manipulate many elements of the story. A common technique is "speaking through sources," where you call people you know are going to give you the quotes and slant you want. Even the choice of the photo an editor chooses to accompany the story can be misleading; catch the subject at the right moment and you can make him appear dejected, angry, or deceptive. We'll show how this is done through examples, words, and pictures. An intriguing avenue to be explored is web journalism. Here's an unregulated Wild West of misinformation, and we'll show how the new technology has compounded an old problem.

Chapter 10: Lawyers

In this chapter, we highlight the tale of a tippy truck, which was documented in a videotape provided by a "safety institute." The tape showed the truck flipping when it took a sharp turn — and the tape showed up on network news. Trial lawyers then showed the report in court when they sued the company. Can you guess who made the tape in the first place? Yes, the "safety institute" was really a group of trial lawyers. Chapter 10 highlights similar shenanigans, including the legal profession's imaginative use of the English language.

Chapter 11: Tobacco Companies

Tobacco companies have a long history of twisting words and burying data. We'll demonstrate the techniques and document the deeds.

Chapter 12: The Auto Industry

This chapter focuses primarily on advertising, but techniques of salespeople deserve some attention here, too. Note that the growth of the leasing industry has spawned many new methods of misrepresentation. We'll look at a typical ad for a leased vehicle and flag the misrepresentations. (My favorite: "Actual price set be dealer." Meaning, literally, that the price on the ad has no meaning.)

Chapter 13: Retail

Did you ever wonder how "fresh squeezed" orange juice can come in a Can it be because "fresh squeezed is ungrammatical and therefore has no enforceable meaning—and can therefore slip into the retailer's lexicon of hollow catch-phrases? Chapter 13 exposes the techniques of deception retail and grocery stores—from bait-and-switch advertising to misleading placement of signs.

Chapter 14: Public Relations

Chapter 14 focuses on how the public relations industry creates false impressions. One of my favorite examples was orchestrated by one of the nation's largest P.R. firms, when it represented the makers of a particular artificial sweetener. Congress was debating whether the substance should be removed from sale because it was a possible carcinogen. The firm arranged for a crowd of diabetic children to crowd the Capitol steps and shriek at congressmen: "We can't eat sugar—please don't take our soft drinks and candy away !" (I'm not making this up, and I can prove it.) We'll detail many instances such as this, including planted book reviews and videotape placed as news.

Chapter 15: Advertising

Advertising is placed at the end of this book part because the field exemplifies our approach toward persuasion, and can therefore be used to illustrate some concluding points. We'll look at the fundamental illogic behind advertising, the way advertisers prod us to make inaccurate conclusions based on misleading information, and how little half-truths are used to propel a big lie.

Any type of proposal should include a positive ending. In this case, I am promising the book will offer solutions, instead of just my grousing.

Part 3: Fighting Back

Chapter 16: Keeping Distortion in Proportion

Chapter 16 provides a guide to how the reader can synthesize the information in the book and stand guard against those who would lie to him or her. The chapter also provides guidance on ways to fight back against people and organizations who mislead you—whom to contact, how to complain, what to ask for.

Chapter 17: Resources: Books, People, and Organizations

The book closes with an extensively annotated bibliography of works that deal with critical thinking and understanding information. Examples include *Language in Thought and Action* by S.I. Hayakawa and *How to Watch TV News* by Neil Postman. Listings of people and associations involved in integrity of information will be included—examples are the various nonprofits involved in analyzing and exposing misleading political ads.

The following section reinforces the credibility of the content.

About the Research Methodology

The author is ideally located at the precise midpoint between Washington and New York. Many of the interviews for the book will take place in those locales. In addition to in-person interview research for the book, the author will also mine:

- newspaper libraries
- videotape collections at New York University and Georgetown University
- collections of papers and tapes at other professional and academic institutions

"Prospectus" is a business-sounding work. In my proposals, I generally include an entirely business-oriented description of the product I am trying to sell. I often close my proposals with a prospectus, a section addressing only sales and markets. In some cases I review competing books and say why mine will meet a section of the market the competitors do not serve.

Prospectus:

Lies We Live By

This prospectus describes the theme, approach, and appeal of *Lies We Live By*, a book that exposes and decodes deception in everyday life. Following this prospectus, a table of contents and a chapter-by-chapter summary detail the subject matter of the work.

Lies We Live By documents how deception has woven itself into our everyday lives—from the ads in the paper to the promises of politicians and even the claims colleges make when they tout "average" SAT scores.

Lies We Live By spotlights the modern technique of telling a "little, lie," a half-truth, a deception based on fine print, hollow word meanings, a statistic with a meaningful component withheld, or a misleading juxtaposition of words and images.

Why This Book?

(In other words, why this book will sell.)

Modern society is inundated with information, and trying to access the flow of knowledge is like taking a drink from a fire hose. Propagandists know that a confused and overwhelmed public is a vulnerable public, and they exploit this information overload with the little lie, the spurious half-truth that looks appealing and seems genuine to a time-starved consumer or voter.

Lying is a *big business*, a *high stakes business*. Investing in stocks, electing a president, choosing a college, leasing a car, booking an airline ticket, all involve a substantial investment of time, trust, and money.

And if you have ever done any of the above, you've been lied to.

Lies We Live By will show how you've been deceived, how you can detect the liar's techniques in the future, and how you can become a resistance fighter for the truth.

The way book publishing usually works is that an editor will like the idea but still have to pitch it to a group of higher-ups. What I do, and what you can do in any persuasive-writing situation, is to provide the pre-packaged sales talk.

What's the Approach?

The over-arching theme of *Lies We Live By* is that deception has become business as usual in the information age. Telling lies taints virtually every transaction into which we enter. And unfortunately, information-glutted Americans have lost what the author so elegantly calls our "crap detector"—the mental device that should start ringing when the truth and the whole truth part company.

Lies We Live By disassembles the business of lying bolt-by-bolt, and shows how the business-as-usual approach has tainted commerce, politics, and education. The book demonstrates how cynical propagandists deliberately mislead the public, hiding behind asterisks, fine print, and tortured statistics.

While the book is spiced with hundreds of amusing anecdotes, it is more than a collection of amusing stories. It cohesively and coherently deals with what I believe is a cancer of modern life, a corrosive practice that eats away a society's connective tissue of trust, truth, and logic.

Every chapter hammers home that point. Every chapter shows how systematic distortion has become business as usual. And the closing chapters of the book tell you how you can fight back.

Why Will Readers Buy This Book?

Here, I address what's in it for the reader. By reader, I mean the person to whom I am trying to sell the book.

Four reasons . . .

One: It is highly promotable. As you can see from the following outline, there are many compelling examples that can compactly be presented on talk shows. Excerpts could be broken out into articles for such publications as *Reader's Digest*. The author is an experienced public speaker and talk show veteran, and delights in administering the public bastinado to corporations and politicians who deserve it. The author is also youthful, handsome, and modest.

Two: It is a good read. In fact, it's funny. Sad, but funny.

Three: The book is at the crest of the first wave of anti-lie, anti-spin public sentiment. Witness the phenomenal success of Howard Kurtz's *The Spin Cycle*.

Four: It is important. The erosion of confidence in the public ethic of honesty undermines the structure of society. If banks lie to us in credit card applications, how can we trust them with our savings? How can we live in a world where every transaction and every statement must be checked for fine print or weasel words? It is current. There is no shortage of examples, and those examples can be updated for new editions. *Lies We Live By* taps into a larger theme of the outrages and frustrations of everyday life—seemingly small things that when added up represent a corrosion of our quality of life. (And topics for a series of future books.) My personal mission is to do what I can to get people thinking about these issues, reacting to them, and fighting back.

—Carl Hausman

An Example of Explaining Complex Information in Simple Terms

Providing clear explanations is one of the biggest challenges in writing, and many jobs—either in part or in whole—deal with clarifying things. Technical writers, financial reporters, political analysts, medical writers, and dozens of other types of professional writers are engaged in this process—which is why I dedicated all of Chapter 6 to the techniques and skills necessary.

Here's a real toughie: How to explain something you can't see. Here is how I and my coauthors, Fritz Messere and Phil Benoit, it in a textbook on audio.

The Basics of Sound

Sound is one of the fundamental senses. It is extraordinary in every sense of the word. Certainly there are some individuals who are unable to hear or have hearing deficiencies. And, for the hearing impaired they often find ways to mitigate this loss, but nothing replaces the ability to hear. For the majority of us, we are blessed with this phenomenal sense that provides us with the ability to speak and hear, to make music, to locate sounds in our environment and to hear the incredible sounds of nature. From the softest of sounds to crashing thunder, sound impacts our daily lives.

The opening is not part of the explanation, of course, but sets a human tone and, it is to be hoped, puts the reader at ease.

A complete discussion about the fundamentals of hearing and audio would fill entire book, but our task here is more limited. We will provide a basic understanding of sound and how it is related to audio and radio.

It's a good idea to set limits at the beginning when explaining something complex. You and the reader know at the outset how far the discussion will go.

There is a certain duality to any discussion of sound. We talk both about hearing sound and reproducing sound.

Sound itself is a vibration—a specific disturbance of air molecules. In order for sound to be transmitted some kind of medium is required. It could be air, water, metal or some other medium. But let's focus on air since that's how we hear most sounds. What happens is this: A sound source (a ringing bell, perhaps) creates changes in air pressure. The ringing bell causes alternating waves of compression (dense dots) and rarefaction (sparse dots) through the air molecules. When air molecules are pushed together, they are said to be in compression. Areas of low pressure, where molecules are pulled apart from one another, are called rarefactions. To visualize the situation, look at Figure 11.3.

The vibration traveling through the air carries information. The way that the ringing bell sounds to our ears is determined by the pattern of vibration. We hear the bell as a result of these air particles crashing into our eardrum. As a matter of fact, the eardrum can be considered a **transducer**. It performs the first step in converting motional energy of vibration into electrical energy transmitted by neurons in the brain.

Italicizing or bolding an unfamiliar word the first time it is used cues the reader to the fact that it is an unusual word that either will be defined or

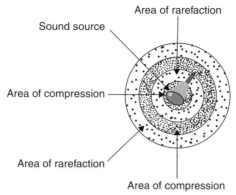

Figure 11.3 **Sound pressure waves emanating from a ringing bell.** Reprinted by permission, Carl Hausman, Fritz Messere, and Philip Benoit, *Modern Radio and Audio Production: Programming and Performance*, 10th ed., Cengage Learning.

should be looked up. In this case, I had a glossary at the end of the book and the reader had been instructed to look up boldface words.

In the audio field there are several common transducers, such as loudspeakers and microphones. Both transduce one form of energy into another. The microphone will convert the motional energy of air particles into electrical energy. That energy then might be transduced into electromechanical energy (via storage in a computer file), send as a broadcast signal (electromagnetically) or it might be transduced back into motional energy by a loudspeaker or headphones.

Most sounds are a complex mixture of different tones but for our discussion we are going to imagine the sound created by a tuning fork. When struck, the tuning fork creates a pure-tone sound that we can represent by a sine wave (see Figure 11.5). This is one of the most frequently used symbols in the world of sound, microphones, and radio—and one of the most frequently misunderstood. A sine wave depicting sound is a graphic representation of the rarefactions and compressions of air molecules. If we were to sample the density of the molecules of a wave (pictured in Figure 11.4), we'd find a thick area, then a thinner area, then a very thin area, then an area somewhat thicker, and then a thick area again. A graph of this pattern would look like the one in Figure 11.5 which is a plot of the sound pattern, not a picture of it. Thus, the sine wave only represents sound. While the sine wave can be used to analyze several fundamental elements of sound, it

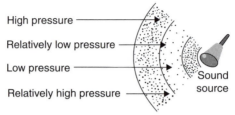

Figure 11.4 Sampling sound pressure waves. Reprinted by permission, Carl Hausman, Fritz Messere, and Philip Benoit, *Modern Radio and Audio Production: Programming and Performance*, 10th ed., Cengage Learning.

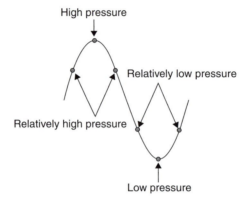

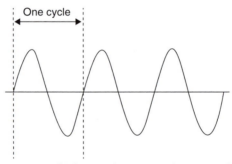

Figure 11.5 A sine wave, which is nothing more than a graph of a sampling of sound pressure waves. Reprinted by permission, Carl Hausman, Fritz Messere, and Philip Benoit, *Modern Radio and Audio Production: Programming and Performance*, 10th ed., Cengage Learning.

really doesn't represent sounds in nature. Most sounds (like your voice or musical instruments) produce many different sounds, not just one pure tone.

Cycle—Each time a wave goes through its pattern and returns to its starting point, it has completed one cycle. A cycle passes through a complete rotation every 360 degrees. The time it takes for a wave to make a complete cycle is called an *interval*.

A cycle can be measured from any starting point. The plot of a cycle is illustrated in Figure 11.5. Note that although a sine wave has 360 degrees in a complete rotation, this representation comprises two equal intervals, called *positive* and *negative intervals*. Each interval is 180 degrees long.

Illustrations are obviously helpful in communicating a complex concept, or in persuasive writing. The key is to keep them simple.

Frequency—Frequency is a measure of how often a cycle is repeated in a given period. Formerly, frequency was described by measuring those rotations or cycles per second (cps). The term *cycles per second* has been replaced by the term **hertz** (Hz), named in honor of the mathematician Heinrich Hertz, who first demonstrated the existence of radio waves. We will see shortly how frequency plays a role in the nature of sound.

It's important to let the reader know that while we are leaving, for a moment, the concept of frequency, we will be coming back to it.

Amplitude—Amplitude is the height of the sine wave. In sound amplitude represents the greatest density of the air particles, so the high point represents the compression of air molecules. In audio it indicates the volume of the sound. The higher the amplitude, the louder the sound.

These elements determine the characteristics of sound, and our sine wave is a visual representation of those characteristics. If nothing else, remember that any sound can be described by one or more sine waves.

I am using frequent headings. Headings are a must in explanatory writing. The reader needs guideposts, and also needs a way to quickly refer back if it is necessary to review.

The Nature of Sound: Frequency

Why did we say "one or more sine waves"? Sounds consist of combinations of wave patterns or waveforms. Although a tuning fork or a device called a *tone generator* will produce, by electronic circuitry, a pure wave (when represented on an oscilloscope), most sounds are really a combination of many waves of different shapes and frequencies and are called *complex waveforms.*

The question-and-answer technique I advocated in the book section on paragraphing comes in handy in explanatory writing.

Frequencies and Your Ears—The human ear can hear very low frequencies from about 35 Hz, like those created by the lowest notes of a pipe organ to extremely high, piercing sounds up to 20,000 Hz. This, of course, depends on the age and health of the ear's owner. Older people generally don't hear high frequencies as well as young people do. The low end of the scale is a deep bass rumbling; the high end is a thin whine that's barely audible to humans.

Example . . . example . . . example.

How Frequency Shapes Sound—A sound is a combination of various waves—some higher, some lower. The fundamental frequency of an average male voice, for example, is typically around 300 Hz. That fundamental frequency is accompanied by secondary frequencies, called overtones. Consonant sounds such as *t* and *d* tend to be much higher than vowels. So while a male voice may be in the 300-Hz range, consonants will raise in pitch, perhaps in the 1,000-Hz range. Very high, hissy consonants, such as *s*, can be well into the 4,000-Hz range, whereas the *th* in *thin* can approach 6,000 Hz. Other components of the sounds of human speech can range as high as 9,000 Hz.

So . . . why are we learning all this? You and I can sense that the reader will be asking this question, so the answer comes next—before the reader tunes out.

The higher-frequency sounds, the consonant sounds, lend intelligibility to speech. If high consonant sounds are not reproduced accurately by any of the transducers in the audio production chain, human speech becomes less intelligible. Also, music that lacks high frequencies tends to sound muddy and dull; the high frequencies add clarity and vibrancy.

Limiting the range of transduced frequencies affects the tone of speech, too. Your older land-line telephones only reproduced frequencies from about 300 to 3,000 Hz. Those older phones had a distinctly nasal quality to their sound. Today's modern cell phones are much better. Using this illustration, you can understand that the differences between speech over low quality and high-quality microphones will be readily apparent to the listener. Various mics reproduce frequencies with varying degrees of effectiveness.

The Nature of Sound: Amplitude

The amplitude of the sine wave represents the volume of the sound. Another way we represent sound volume is by measuring it in *decibels*. A decibel (dB) is a very complex measurement of *relative* sound levels. (The decibel is really a measure of one-tenth of a Bel, an audio measure originally used by audiologists.) While decibels are measured in a logarithmic scale, you only need to remember two essential points about decibels:

> *Sometimes you just have to give up and admit you can't really explain the subject fully and give examples. Understanding decibels requires a very good grasp of higher math; so examples will have to suffice. This is important: NOT EVERYTHING NEEDS TO BE FULLY EXPLAINED. If you are getting into a subject that is too deep for the reader, and there is really no reason for the reader to know the intricacies, give a few "for examples" and move on.*

1. The higher the decibel reading, the louder the sound. Thus, 20 dB is the sound level of a whisper in a very quiet room; a 55 dB would be the sound level of normal conversational speech; 75 dB is the noise level in city traffic; 110 dB is a loud, amplified rock band; and 140 dB is a jet engine at takeoff. Sustained loud sounds above 110 dB can actually damage your hearing. (These measurements are expressed in a particular form called *dB SPL*—decibel sound pressure level.)
2. The ear does not hear all sounds in a linear way. It is believed that an increase or decrease of 1 to 2 dB SPL is the smallest change in sound level a human can perceive, but an increase of 6 dB SPL is what the most people perceive as a doubling of the sound's volume. (Try this out next time you're at an audio board. When a steady sound such as tone moves from –6 up to 0 on a VU meter, does the apparent loudness of the sound seem to double?)

> *Next, another direct question to revive the reader's attention . . .*

So why do we use decibels? You would normally think that when you double the power output of a sound, it would increase proportionally. However, as we noted before the ear does not hear in a linear fashion. For example, if you were playing music on a stereo at a level equal to 10 watts of power and you turned it up to a level equal to an output of 15 watts (an addition of 5 watts), you would not perceive the increase as being 1.5 times the original volume. Because it is difficult to measure relative volume by talking about power, such as watts (e.g. an amplifier has an output of x watts), we use a measurement system that measures sound in a way that corresponds to the way the ear appears to hear sound. Hence, the decibel is a very useful tool to measure significant increases or decreases in apparent volume.

Most audio and radio consoles have visual indicators to help the operator "see" the audio output. Some audio consoles simply use LEDs to show good (green) and distorted (red) levels. Broadcasters often use VU (Volume Unit) meters that frequently have gradations measured in decibels. In radio, we have standardized 0 VU to equal a relative sound level that will power our transmitter and/or provide a proper level to our recording devices. Anything less than 0 dB (100 percent) will represent some number that is lower than the maximum level. Using this scheme, we don't have to work with large decibel numbers. Remember, the 0 dB reading is relative. Once we set 0 as our maximum level we can simply look and see if our audio levels are okay, low or high. A VU meter reading of −3 means that your input is 3 dB lower than the optimum level and a level that is +3 means that your level is 3 dB higher than optimal.

You don't have Chapter 3, of course, but should you be captivated by this subject just do a web search on "VU Meters."

Other Characteristics of Sound

We've pretty well covered the physical properties that make up the nature of sound, but some other areas are also worth considering.

This is an "internal summary." It cues the reader that we are done with discussing the physical properties and are moving on to a discussion of pitch, duration, and other characteristics.

Pitch, a term commonly used to describe sound, is not the same thing as frequency. Frequency is a physical measurement denoting the number of complete sound vibrations over a period of time (e.g. Hertz, cycles per second) while pitch is the ear's and mind's subjective interpretation of frequency plus loudness, signifying the way we hear a frequency. The term, pitch, is more commonly used in music and is often referred to as an assign tone on a musical scale. The human ear just doesn't hear the same way a scientific instrument does. For example, try this experiment. Listen to a siren approaching. As sound gets closer to us, its apparent pitch *rises*, but in actuality its frequency doesn't change!

Good example, if I do say so myself . . . and I do. Again, examples add a tremendous amount of understanding to complex subjects.

Duration is also a characteristic of sound, too. It refers to the amount of time a sound exists and to the amount of time individual harmonics exist within a complex waveform. This may sound complex initially, but think of plucking a guitar string. If you pluck it hard, it can vibrate for several seconds. During that time, the frequency stays the same but the sound level decreases until the string stops vibrating.

Another example. This is a pretty complicated subject, but everyone understands what a guitar string does, and now everyone understands at least something about sound duration.

Velocity and distance also play a role in the way we hear sound. Sound is not very fast; it travels through air at only a little more than 1,100 feet per second, or about 750 miles per hour. Sound travels at different rates through different media; it travels about four times faster through water, for example. However, sound has to vibrate through a medium such as air or water; there's no sound in a vacuum.

The relative slowness of sound in air can be illustrated by a familiar example. When sitting in the bleachers during a baseball game, you will see the batter complete his swing before you hear the crack of the bat hitting the ball. Because of the slowness of sound, you can perceive echoes (the immediate bounce back of sound) and reverberation (the continued bouncing of sound) in an enclosure with reflective walls. A large room with reflective walls will make the reverberations take longer to *decay*, or die out. Do you like to sing in the shower? The reverberation time in small tiled enclosures is very short and the reverberation makes your voice sound fuller and more powerful. We do need to point out that the speed of sound is different than that of audio, the electronic reproduction of sound. Audio in electronic circuits travels at the speed of light, about 186,000 miles per second.

See that pattern? After every introduction of an unfamiliar concept there is an example. You don't need to do this with all explanatory writing, of course, but in highly technical explanations it's essential.

Distance also makes a difference in how loud the sound is when it reaches us. As a sound travels through the open air, it loses its intensity. When sound travels two times a specified distance, it arrives at only one-quarter of its original intensity. This behavior is said to comply with the inverse square law. This means that the intensity of a sound varies inversely with the square of the distance. For example, in an open-air environment as the distance between you and a sound source doubles, the sound intensity will reduce by a factor of 4.

A final characteristic is the sound's quality, or *timbre*. This, again, is a factor in how we perceive sound. Timbre has to do with the way harmonics of a sound are combined and with the relative intensities of those harmonics. Those combinations make us perceive a difference between middle C played on a piano and the same note played on a trumpet. The striking of the string on a piano produces a different set of harmonics (overtones) than those produced by air passing through a valve on a trumpet. Our ears can easily recognize the timbre of a diverse range of musical instruments, along with many different sounds in nature.

Another example the layperson can relate to. Everybody knows the difference in sound quality between a trumpet and a piano.

Summary of the Basics of Sound

Understanding how sound behaves is a prerequisite to learning about transducers, particularly microphones, and much of what you need to know concerns how a mic reproduces sound.

Sound is a vibration of molecules in the air, and it consists of rarefactions and compressions. A sine wave is a graphic representation of a sound wave; it is not supposed to be a picture of the wave.

Sound is measured in terms of frequency and amplitude. Frequency, which tells how often in a given period the sound wave makes a complete cycle, is measured in cycles per second, now called *hertz*.

Amplitude is the height of the sine wave. It refers to the loudness of the sound and is measured in decibels (dBs). Sound travels through air at about 1,100 feet per second.

Characteristics of sound include pitch (the way we perceive frequency), loudness (the way we perceive volume), and quality or timbre (the way we interpret the complex waveforms). Duration refers to how long a sound lasts.[4]

It's very helpful to provide a summary at the end of a section of technical explanation.

Example of a Blog Post That Gets the Company's Point Across While at the Same Time Entertaining the Reader

This is from the corporate blog of the same firm that produced the press release I reprinted earlier. The firm, which consults on web use measurement, among other services, is run by someone who happens to be not only a fine writer but a part-time standup comedian.

Note how the writing is engaging and informal, and relates some interesting social commentary to the firm's core mission.

You can see the original blog post at https://blog.rjmetrics.com/2014/09/03/the-ice-bucket-challenge-data-debrief-who-dumped-who-donated-and-was-it-all-worth-it/.

The parts reproduced here in bold are actually links on the web version of this release.

This time last month, you'd probably never heard of the ice bucket challenge. Since then, it has grown into **one of the most successful viral marketing campaigns of all time**, and we've all been . . . well . . . doused.

The phenomenon has **sparked a series of hilarious fails**, inspired a new genre of bucket challenges, and **garnered a fair share of criticism**. It has also **raised over $100 million since July 29** for Amyotrophic Lateral Sclerosis (ALS), an astonishing 3,504% increase over donations during this same period last year.

Notice how gracefully the links have been integrated into the copy.

With the barrage of videos slowly working their way out of our Facebook feeds, we decided it was finally time to take a look back at the data behind the ice bucket challenge. We downloaded and profiled a 1,500 randomly-selected #icebucketchallenge videos using the YouTube API, and then uploaded the raw data to RJMetrics for analysis.

(If you'd like to try RJMetrics for your own business, **click at** https://rjmetrics.com/signup/cloudbi for a 14 day free trial.)

Our complete findings, which also provide some insights into the allegations of "slacktivism," are included below. Here are some highlights:

- 20% of participants took the challenge indoors
- Participants were 2x more likely to be male than female
- 1 in 4 participants didn't even mention ALS in their video
- Only 1 in 5 participants mentioned a donation

Taking a Look at the Basics

Dumping a bucket of ice and water on one's head is an activity best suited for the outdoors. Yet almost 10% chose an indoor, non-bathtub environment.

Headings break up content on the page. Also, the short paragraphs highlight the points of the analysis.

During the course of our research we noticed another unmistakable trend: the majority of those getting iced were males. Women made up about 30% of participants in the challenge.

Surprising gender breakdown of the #icebucketchallenge http://ow.ly/B2aFB pic.twitter.com/TuGkO2RI8C

TWEET THIS

Ice bucket fails have already become a genre of their own, with many of the best involving a "helper" who accidentally drops the bucket on the person's head. **Oops!** We were curious how many people did the dumping themselves vs. recruited some help. It was a close split with only a small majority (53%) electing to have someone dump the bucket for them.

Slacktivism or Successive Approximations?

With our basic curiosities appeased, we set out to address some tougher questions.

One of the harshest criticisms leveraged against the campaign is that it's just another example of "**slacktivism**". This relatively new term is associated with philanthropic half-measures in which contributors feel satisfied to donate with their tweets and shares rather than their wallets. More extreme versions of the argument claim that these slacktivists are more focused on bringing attention to themselves than to a charitable cause.

Clever . . . the introduction of a new term—slacktivism.

Also, note how the authors cleverly set up buttons on the page to make it easy for readers to Tweet content from the blog.

There is certainly some data to uphold this claim: a whopping **26% of participants didn't even mention ALS in their videos.** And **a paltry 20% of participants mentioned donating money.**
A whopping 26% didn't mention ALS in their #icebucketchallenge videos. http://ow.ly/B2aFB pic.twitter.com/Zc0b521DAw

TWEET THIS

Only 20% of participants mentioned making a donation in their #icebucketchallenge videos. http://ow.ly/B2aFB pic.twitter.com/ 5VoXDGMew9

TWEET THIS

So was this whole thing just a big waste of time? Hardly. Don't forget about that $100 Million! With a 20% conversion rate from dumper to donor, this campaign was still able to generate some serious cash thanks to the size of its reach.

Even with the slacktivists slacking away, the campaign worked because, for enough people, it "hooked" something deep in their psychology. By getting our attention with an entertaining video and a simple message, the campaign moved millions of people one step closer to donating than they would have been otherwise.

OK . . . and here is the main point. This is the place where the needs of the writer and the needs of the reader intersect.

This phenomenon is known as "successive approximations", or more commonly as **the-foot-in-the-door technique**. The gist is that, by getting people to make a small commitment, they become emotionally invested and more likely to make a bigger commitment.

Instead of heading straight to a call to donate, the ice bucket challenge asks people to take a series of small steps:

- Step 1: Participate in the ice bucket challenge
- Step 2: Mention ALS
- Step 3: Donate money
- Step 4: Publicly call out your friends to do the same

This technique escalates commitment, and the data shows it:

Participants who mentioned ALS were 5x more likely to donate, doing so 25% of the time vs. just 5% for those who didn't mention the cause.

People who mention ALS in #icebucketchallenge videos 5x more likely to donate. http://ow.ly/B2aFB

TWEET THIS

Participants who donated were 12% more likely to nominate their friends, doing so at 89% vs. 79% for non-donators. **They also nominated 29% more people on average**: donators nominated 3.98 people where non-donators nominated 3.09 people.

The data couldn't be more clear: **the strategy of escalating commitment works**. At every stage in the ice bucket challenge process, people who participated in the prior stage are more likely to continue participating.

Secret to #icebucketchallenge success?: "escalating commitment" strategy http://ow.ly/B2aFB

TWEET THIS

Was It Worth It?

So, were there slacktivists participating in the ice bucket challenge? Absolutely, but passive consumers are the byproduct of any conversion funnel. The slacktivists are "exhaust" that is generated by creating new donors and raising awareness. Not a bad tradeoff in my opinion.

And it ends with a good, clear, satisfying summary.

The ice bucket challenge has raised $100 million for ALSA while growing our collective awareness for a rare, painful disease. In addition, the very nature of successive approximations suggests that those who completed each of these small steps will continue to feel an emotional investment in the future success of ALS research. We'll raise a bucket to that.

About the Author

Robert J. Moore
CEO and Co-Founder, RJMetrics
Robert Moore is the co-founder and CEO of RJMetrics. His explorations in data have covered everything from figuring out why our logo looked like underpants to understanding Pinterest's $3.8B valuation. Bob is also an amateur improv comic, an advocate of the Philadelphia tech scene, and a regular contributor to the *New York Times* small business blog.

Again, always stress the author's credibility. It makes your piece more impactful and builds your brand.[5]

Notes

CHAPTER 3

1. George Orwell, "A Hanging," *The Adelphi,* August 1931, http://www
.public-domain-poetry.com/stories/george-orwell-eric-arthur-blair/a-
hanging-1051

CHAPTER 4

1. David Hanners, "Kicking Tin: The Search for Pieces," in Kendall
J. Wills, ed., *The Pulitzer Prizes* (New York: Simon and Schuster, 1989), 456.

2. Troy Patterson, "The Trivago Guy," *Slate,* accessed October 31, 2015,
http://www.slate.com/blogs/browbeat/2014/08/05/trivago_guy_what_
modern_men_can_learn_from_this_enigmatic_weirdo.html

3. William Shakespeare, *As You Like It*, Act II, Scene 7, Poets.org, accessed
October 31, 2015, https://www.poets.org/poetsorg/poem/you-it-act-ii-
scene-vii-all-worlds-stage

4. William Shakespeare, *The Tragedy of Macbeth*, Act V, Scene 5.

5. A. E. Housman, "Loveliest of Trees the Cherry Now," in Louis Unter-
meyer, ed., *Modern British Poetry* (New York: Harcourt, Brace and Howe, 1920),
Bartleby.com, accessed October 31, 2015, http://www.bartleby.com/123/2.html

6. Edward R. Murrow, cited in Norman Finkelstein, *With Heroic Truth,
The Life of Edward R. Murrow* (Boston: Houghton Mifflin Harcourt, 1997).

7. Mark Forsyth, *The Elements of Eloquence: How to Turn the Perfect English Phrase* (London: Icon, 2013), Kindle edition.

8. Hanners, "Kicking Tin," 456.

9. Samuel Taylor Coleridge, "The Rime of the Ancient Mariner," in Sir Arthur Thomas Quiller-Couch, ed., *The Oxford Book of English Verse* (Oxford: Clarendon, 1919, [c1901]).

10. The bartender says, "Hey, pal, why the long face?" Don't blame me; I told you it wouldn't work.

11. Adlai Stevenson, in *Adlai Stevenson of Illinois: A Portrait*, archive. org, accessed October 31, 2015, http://archive.org/stream/adlaiestevenso no012929mbp/adlaiestevensono012929mbp_djvu.txt

12. Jennifer Ordonez, "Cash Cows: Burger Joints Call Them 'Heavy Users,' But Not to Their Faces," *The Wall Street Journal*, updated January 12, 2000, accessed October 31, 2015, https://www.google.com/url?sa=t&rct= j&q=&esrc=s&source=web&cd=1&cad=rja&uact=8&ved=0CB0QFjAAa hUKEwjhvcPZuO_IAhXOuB4KHaCKA9Q&url=http%3A%2F%2Fwww .wsj.com%2Farticles%2FSB947636708123070129&usg=AFQjCNHe5dKBb YVOO5IJ9pef9UY0-tC_Ag&bvm=bv.106379543,d.eWE

CHAPTER 5

1. "Tips for Writers," *Miami Herald*, accessed September 18, 2015, http://www.miamiherald.com/living/liv-columns-blogs/dave-barry/article 1936919.html#storylink=cpy

2. "Dangle These in Front of a Grammarian!" accessed September 18, 2015, http://sinandsyntax.com/blog/dangling-modifiers/

CHAPTER 6

1. "Dark, Perhaps Forever," *New York Times*, accessed September 18, 2015, http://www.nytimes.com/2008/06/03/science/03dark.html?pagewanted=all

2. "The Conversation I Never Had," *Medium*, accessed September 18, 2015, https://medium.com/the-lighthouse/the-conversation-i-never-had-d2428866f0d3. Reprinted with permission.

3. James C. Humes, *Speak Like Churchill, Stand Like Lincoln: 21 Powerful Secrets of History's Greatest Speakers* (New York: Three Rivers Press, 2002), Kindle Edition.

4. Ibid.

5. "The Real War," *Atlantic*, accessed September 18, 2015, https://www .theatlantic.com/past/docs/unbound/bookauth/battle/fussell.htm

CHAPTER 7

1. "Honoring Copyrights Should Be Simple Decency," *Chronicle of Higher Education*, accessed September 18, 2015, http://chronicle.com/article/ Honoring-Copyrights-Should-Be/86635/

2. Ibid.

3. "The Greatest Sales Letter of All Time," accessed September 18, 2015, http://www.copyblogger.com/the-greatest-sales-letter-of-all-time/

4. "Privacy, Profit, and Purpose," accessed September 18, 2015, http://carlhausman.com/2012/02/27/privacy-profit-and-purpose/

5. Ibid.

CHAPTER 8

1. *Time*, February 13, 2005.

2. P. J. O'Rourke, *Republican Party Reptile* (New York: Grove, 1987), 79.

3. Orwell, "A Hanging."

CHAPTER 10

1. Daniel Coyle, *The Little Book of Talent: 52 Tips for Improving Your Skills* (New York: Bantam, 2012), Kindle edition.

2. "The Pocket Notebooks of 20 Famous Men," *The Art of Manliness*, accessed September 18, 2015, http://www.artofmanliness.com/2010/09/13/the-pocket-notebooks-of-20-famous-men/

CHAPTER 11

1. Carl Hausman, "George Eastman," *Media History Digest*, Fall/Winter, 1988, 8–16, 39. Reprinted with permission.

2. Orwell, "A Hanging."

3. "Lessons from Lyin' Brian: It's Time to Reinvent TV News," *Medium*, accessed September 18, 2015, https://medium.com/@carlhausman/lessons-from-lyin-brian-it-s-time-to-reinvent-tv-news-21b1cb4c247f. Reprinted with permission.

4. Carl Hausman, Fritz Messere, Philip Benoit, and Lewis B. O'Donnell, *Modern Radio and Audio Production: Programming and Performance*, 10th Edition (Boston: Cengage, 2015), eBook edition. Copyright © 2016 Wadsworth, a part of Cengage Learning, Inc. Reproduced by permission. www.cengage.com/permissions.

5. Robert J. Moore, "The Ice Bucket Challenge Data Debrief: Who Dumped, Who Donated, and Was It All Worth It?" *RJ Metrics Blog*, September 3, 2014, https://blog.rjmetrics.com/2014/09/03/the-ice-bucket-challenge-data-debrief-who-dumped-who-donated-and-was-it-all-worth-it/. Reprinted with permission.

Suggested Readings

Here are some excellent books you'll find helpful. Because books are republished frequently in many formats, I'll just list the author and title.

Alicia Abell, *Business Grammar, Style & Usage: The Most Used Desk Reference for Articulate and Polished Business Writing and Speaking by Executives Worldwide.*

James C. Humes, *Speak Like Churchill, Stand Like Lincoln: 21 Powerful Secrets of History's Greatest Speakers.*

Michael Hyatt, *Platform: Get Noticed in a Noisy World.*

Stephen King, *On Writing: A Memoir of the Craft.*

Michael E. Larson, *How to Write a Book Proposal.*

Anatoly Lieberman, *Word Origins and How We Know Them.*

Sean Platt and Johnny B. Truant, with David Wright, *Write. Publish. Repeat. (The No-Luck-Required Guide to Self-Publishing Success).*

Susan Rabiner and Alfred Fortunato, *Thinking Like Your Editor: How to Write Great Serious Nonfiction and Get It Published.*

William Strunk and E. B. White, *The Elements of Style.*

Susan Thurman, *The Only Grammar Book You'll Ever Need.*

Index

About the Author

CARL HAUSMAN, Ph.D., is the author of 20 books and hundreds of published articles.

Hausman is professor of journalism at Rowan University in New Jersey. He has taught and developed a variety of writing courses and is national chair of the broadcast journalism judging panel for the National Headliner Awards, one of the nation's oldest and largest awards programs recognizing journalism excellence.

He also writes commentary and has been a guest on national and local broadcast and cable programs including *The O'Reilly Factor*, Anderson Cooper's *World News Now*, and CBS's *Capitol Voices*.

When not coyly writing about himself in the third person, Hausman also consults with individuals and organizations on effective communication skills.

His blog and website are at www.CarlHausman.com.